THE NEW LONG LIFE

THE NEW LONG LIFE

*A Framework for Flourishing in a
Changing World*

ANDREW J. SCOTT AND
LYNDA GRATTON

BLOOMSBURY PUBLISHING
LONDON · OXFORD · NEW YORK · NEW DELHI · SYDNEY

BLOOMSBURY PUBLISHING
Bloomsbury Publishing Plc
50 Bedford Square, London, WC1B 3DP, UK

BLOOMSBURY, BLOOMSBURY PUBLISHING and the Diana logo are
trademarks of Bloomsbury Publishing Plc

First published in Great Britain 2020

Images designed by Thomas Bohm, User Design, Illustration and Typesetting
and White Halo Design

Lynda Gratton and Andrew J. Scott have asserted their right under the Copyright,
Designs and Patents Act, 1988, to be identified as Authors of this work

For legal purposes the Image Credits on pp. 229–30 constitute an extension
of this copyright page

A catalogue record for this book is available from the British Library

Library of Congress Cataloguing-in-Publication data has been applied for

ISBN: HB: 978-1-5266-1518-3; TPB: 978-1-5266-1517-6; eBook: 978-1-5266-1519-0

4 6 8 10 9 7 5 3

Typeset by Newgen KnowledgeWorks Pvt. Ltd., Chennai, India
Printed and bound in Great Britain by CPI Group (UK) Ltd, Croydon CR0 4YY

To find out more about our authors and books visit www.bloomsbury.com
and sign up for our newsletters

To Diane & Nigel,
Our partners in a new long life

CONTENTS

INTRODUCTION

Human history is an impressive tale of collective achievement. Over thousands of years we have substantially increased our numbers, our lifespan and the resources available to us. We are today far richer and far healthier as a consequence.

Human ingenuity is at the heart of this progress, bringing improvements in knowledge that, embedded in new technologies and education, creates new possibilities and new opportunities. Fire, agriculture, writing, mathematics, the printing press, the steam engine, electricity, penicillin and computers are just some of the innovations that have propelled our standard of living upward.

While human ingenuity has driven these improvements, progress has not always been smooth or swift. Sometimes it is painful, protracted and tumultuous – both for individuals and for society.

Take for example the switch around 10,000 years ago from foraging to farming. In the long run people became richer and healthier, but the transition to the new technologies of farming created a drop in living standards that persisted for centuries. During the UK's Industrial Revolution a similar lag occurred, when living standards failed to improve for many in the first few decades of technological disruption. The human burden wasn't just economic, it was also psychological. As a consequence of industrialisation people relocated away from their families and traditional communities into fast-growing cities, often lacking support and security. They also had to learn new skills, adopt novel roles and identities and often alienating ways of working.

For many experiencing this transition, a sense of progress would have felt very distant.

Both these transitions share a common pattern: human ingenuity created technological advances which undermined existing economic and social structures which, in response, required a different form of human ingenuity – *social ingenuity*. If technological ingenuity creates new possibilities based on new knowledge; then social ingenuity devises ways of living that enable these inventions to improve collectively, and individually, the human lot.

But importantly, social ingenuity does not automatically flow from technological ingenuity. And without social ingenuity, technological ingenuity does not bring unalloyed benefits. That is why the historical pattern of progress and improvement is more evident viewed in retrospect than through the perspective of those experiencing the shift. It is also why periods – when a gap appears between these two types of ingenuity – are characterised by anxiety, transition and social experimentation.

THE FRANKENSTEIN SYNDROME

We are living through a period where the gap between technological and social ingenuity is growing wider. Technological ingenuity is racing ahead, but social ingenuity is lagging and as a result our social forms – the structures and systems that are the context of our lives – have not yet caught up. We might be dazzled by the imminent promise of what technology can achieve, but we are anxious about the social consequences.

In Mary Shelley's novel *Frankenstein*, the creation of Dr Victor Frankenstein rebels and kills his maker. Today there is also a sense of a 'Frankenstein syndrome', fears that our very own human technological triumphs will rise up against us and create not human progress but human misery. In other words, that technological ingenuity is about to manifest itself so powerfully and rapidly it will overwhelm our way of living and we run the risk of losing our jobs, our livelihoods and even our sense of what it is to be human.

Media stories are full of such warnings – '800 million jobs lost globally through automation by 2030',[1] 'more than half of US jobs at risk'.[2] And these fears are not just economic, they are also existential. Stephen Hawking believed: 'The development of full [Generalised Artificial] intelligence could spell the end of the human race' – a fear shared by figures including Bill Gates and Elon Musk. Shelley's novel is a cautionary tale of human knowledge and ingenuity.

Concerns around human ingenuity are not simply restricted to technology. There is also a profound unease about longevity. During the twentieth century, human ingenuity, through major public health improvements and staggering medical developments, significantly increased the length of life. At the beginning of the century a girl born in the UK could expect a lifespan of around fifty-two years; by the end of the century this had increased to eighty-one years – (and by 2010, eighty-three). By 2050 there will be more than 438 million people in China over the age of sixty-five (that's more than the current population of the US); in Japan 1 in 5 people will be over the age of eighty. But rather than celebrate these extraordinary achievements, the fear is that an aging society will bankrupt countries, destroy pensions, increase health costs and lead inevitably to a weaker economy. We fear human ingenuity and worry that the advancement of knowledge will undermine human life and well-being.

These concerns about human achievements backfiring are understandable but we believe they are also limiting. Given the historical record, surely there are ways that can be found to ensure that humanity benefits? Shouldn't smart new technologies and longer, healthier lives be considered opportunities and not problems? In the words of Joseph Coughlin, head of AgeLab at Massachusetts Institute of Technology (MIT): 'The greatest achievement in the history of humankind, and all we can say is, is it going to make Medicare go broke? Why don't we take that and create new stories, new rituals and new mythologies for people as they age?'[3]

The challenge is that for these benefits to be really felt, social ingenuity must be as widespread and as profound and innovative as technological ingenuity. That means each of us must be ingenious: be prepared to question norms, create new ways of living, build deeper insights, experiment and explore. And that also means that our institutions – be they governments, education or corporations – must also rise to the challenge of social ingenuity.

It is this need for social ingenuity that is the fundamental motivation for us writing this book. Our hope is to ignite a conversation about what it is we as humans would like to achieve in response to new technologies and longer lives and how we might seek to flourish in the coming decades. We want to support you as you consider what is likely to happen in the years ahead; to intrigue you about the forms social ingenuity could take; and to provide you with the tools to proactively navigate the transitions and upheavals that we are all experiencing.

SOCIAL PIONEERS

Discussions about how our future will be transformed invariably focus on the phenomena of 'the rise of the robots' and an 'aging society'. What is noticeable about these expressions is how *impersonal* they are. They are about machines or about 'the other'. Yet the human ingenuity required to make these developments work for all of us will be fundamentally *personal*.

That is because the seemingly impersonal aggregate trends of longevity and technology are exerting an enormous impact on what it means to be human. As we will show, they are shaping when and if we marry, the ways we combine family with work and distribute tasks between genders; what we learn, how we learn and who we learn from; how we think of our careers and jobs and piece together our working identity; what we do at each stage of our lives and how we construct a life narrative.

These fundamentals of human life are inevitably changing. The question you face is: What is it you want them to change to?

With millions of others facing the same dilemmas and asking the same questions, this is now becoming fertile ground for social ingenuity. What is clear is the past will not be a good guide to the future. The traditional choices of past generations are unlikely to be appropriate; and the social structures that traditionally served as the framework for living may no longer be capable of delivering. You will need to both understand these trends and also have the courage and motivation to act on this knowledge. Whatever your age, as longevity and technology place us in novel circumstances, we need to be prepared to experiment as individuals but also collectively as families, as corporations, as educators and as governments.

We must all be prepared to be social pioneers: this is the message at the heart of this book.

EVERYBODIES

We view these changing circumstances through the eyes of a cast of fictional characters – our 'everybodies'. Our hope is that through them you will be able to forge deeper insight into your own life as well as draw connections between broader social trends and your own choices.

Our 'everybodies' are:

Hiroki and Madoka: a young mid-twenties Japanese couple living in the city of Kanazawa who are looking for a new way of living as a couple over a long life but feeling constrained by their parents and societal expectations.

Radhika: a single college graduate in her late twenties working as a professional freelancer in Mumbai. She is enjoying the freedom of the gig economy and has already defied social norms, but realises she has tough choices ahead of her.

Estelle: a thirty-year-old single parent with two children. She works part-time as a cashier in a high-street supermarket chain in London, and in the evenings works in a local nursing home. She would like more regular and stable work.

Tom: a forty-year-old truck driver from Dallas, Texas, who lives with his wife and adult son. He is keeping abreast of developments in the technology of autonomous vehicles and is wondering what impact this will have on his job.

Ying: a divorced fifty-five-year-old accountant in Sydney, who has just heard that she has lost her job. The work is being automated and her age and length of service make her too expensive to keep on. She needs to work for financial reasons and feels she has many more productive years left in her career.

Clive: a seventy-one-year-old retired engineer living just outside Birmingham in the UK. He retired at sixty-five and is enjoying life with his wife and family, including four grandchildren. He worries about managing his finances in retirement and hopes to re-engage with work as well as his local community.

OUR PROPOSITION

The genesis of this book began with the many conversations we had following the success of our previous work, *The 100-Year Life – Living and Working in an Age of Longevity*. We discovered that whilst people talked about the impact of longer lives, invariably it was the *combination* of technology and longevity that was the source of many questions: as careers lengthened, where would jobs come from? Would robots take away our jobs? What would this mean for careers and the different stages of life? It seemed to us that although we had advanced a more positive agenda around 'aging', there were deep fears and concerns around technology that needed to be addressed. Avoiding the Frankenstein syndrome is hard.

Our hope is that our combined perspectives of an economist and a psychologist will provide a breadth of insight needed to more fully explore the interactions between technology and longevity and the social ingenuity required to ensure humanity can flourish. In Part I: Human Questions, we explore the interaction between technology and longevity by examining the staggering recent achievements in Artificial Intelligence (AI) and robotics, considering the trends in life expectancy and health and then reviewing how society is aging. We use our everybodies as a lens to imagine the questions these developments trigger and the set of choices they create. These achievements impact significantly on how we construct ways of living that enable human flourishing. In other words, they are a profound invitation to social ingenuity.

The crucial question though is social ingenuity for what purpose? Clearly the overarching aim is to achieve human flourishing. But how do we design new social forms? and on what basis will these social forms be judged? Economic prosperity has to be a part, and we must think about how we can build the resources to finance a good life. However, any positive social reform should fundamentally be capable of delivering on deeper aspects of what it means to be human: to support the development of a cohesive and positive human narrative; to enable people to explore, to experiment and to learn; and to build and sustain relationships with others. These three principles of Narrate, Explore and Relate form the basis for the analysis laid out in Part II: Human Ingenuity, which outlines the steps each of us needs to take to adjust to this new long life.

As we outline in Part II, there is much that you as a social pioneer can achieve on your own. Yet the choices you face and the decisions you make are embedded in a wider context of partnerships and interactions. This holds especially true for your interactions with educational institutions, companies and governments. In order for everyone to flourish there needs to be significant institutional change, and in Part III: Human Society, we lay out the deep-seated changes that need to occur to our economic and social system. There is an immense pressure for change, an agenda that is becoming clearer, and a profound need for both individual and collective action.

PART ONE

HUMAN QUESTIONS

1

HUMAN PROGRESS

Whether it's using a wheel or boiling a kettle, across history humans have used technology to make their lives easier. For each generation the word 'technology' is assigned to unfamiliar new developments – those they imagine will usher in a new age.[1] Today we use it most often in connection with computers which, powered by a quartet of 'laws', are seeing their abilities transformed.

CREATING EXTRAORDINARY TECHNOLOGY

In 1965 the co-founder of Intel, Gordon Moore, conjectured that computing power[2] would double every eighteen months. This observation, 'Moore's Law', has proved to be remarkably accurate and with this dramatic increase in power has come a host of innovations, including autonomous vehicles. If this exponential growth holds, then in the next three years the computational power of autonomous vehicles will rise a further fourfold – making today's versions look rudimentary and limited.

It seems that the world around us is on the verge of being transformed by machines that are improving at a staggering rate. But will Moore's Law continue? The technological challenge is increasing the number of processing units on a chip, which are now so small that the limits of nanotechnology are being reached, threatening a slowdown in the rate of increase. Some experts are forecasting that Moore's Law will even come to an end within the next five years.

The irony is that even as growth in computing power is feared to be slowing, belief in the technological power of AI and robotics has sped up. Parallel technological developments are exploiting the gains Moore's Law has already achieved and it is the combined impact of these new technologies that will reshape the economy, the work you do and how you live your life.

One of these complementary technologies is the size of the bandwidth through which information can be distributed. The American technologist George Gilder predicts that bandwidth will grow at least three times the pace of computing power. This 'Gilder's Law' implies that if computing power doubles every eighteen months, then bandwidth doubles every six months. The result has been an explosive growth in Internet traffic. By 2018 this was estimated at 1.8 zettabytes[3] – substantially more than all the words humans have written in their entire history.

When bandwidth grows, so the numbers of network connections increases. As Robert Metcalfe, the inventor of the Ethernet, observed in 'Metcalfe's Law', the value of a network rises in proportion to the *square* of connected users. That means if the number of connected users doubles, the value of the network rises more than fourfold. This explains the astonishing expansion of Facebook and YouTube – the bigger the network, the more attractive it becomes to new users.

What supercharges this growth even further is an observation by Hal Varian, chief economist at Google.[4] 'Varian's Law' explains how the sheer breadth of freely available existing technologies creates the possibilities of valuable combinations of existing ideas. For instance, driverless cars in some sense require no new technologies but just 'mash-ups' of existing technologies such as 'GPS, Wi-Fi, advanced sensors, anti-lock brakes, automatic transmission, traction and stability control, adaptive cruise control, lane control, and mapping software'.[5] The more such technologies exist, the wider the variety of mash-ups available to exploit, and the more valuable the combinations – and, as a consequence, the more rapidly entrepreneurs will seek to bring them to market.

It is this combination of the underlying technological capabilities described in Moore's, Gilder's, Metcalfe's and Varian's laws that is bringing about the unprecedented and accelerating developments in robotics and Artificial Intelligence. The result isn't just new products, but also new ways of operating, the emergence of new sectors of the economy and shifts in value, and a dramatic change in the nature of the jobs that are available.

Will machines take our jobs?

Tom drives a truck in Texas and is hearing more about autonomous vehicles. He knows something about them and has even seen them on occasion moving around the streets where he lives. During his working life he has already experienced major changes to the navigation, tracking and fuel efficiency systems of the trucks he drives – but this time it feels different. He is aware of the investments being made by leading technology companies such as Alphabet, and automotive companies like BMW and Tesla, and ride share companies such as Uber. By October 2018, Alphabet's self-driving car Waymo had already racked up more than 10 million miles of driving on public roads.

Tom's home state of Texas is one of twenty-two US states that have already embraced regulations which allow autonomous driving test runs as a precursor to possible full-scale adoption. It seems to him more a matter of *when* and not *if* autonomous vehicles will become mainstream. He has also read the early press releases from the investors in autonomous vehicles; these claim that compared to humans, autonomous vehicles are more reliable, less error prone and have no need of a break. When drivers' pay and benefits account for nearly 40 per cent of shipping companies' costs, the economic incentives behind autonomous vehicles are obvious. There are also broader social benefits: in the US, over 4,000 people are killed each year in crashes involving trucks.

All of this makes Tom nervous about the future of his job – along with many of the estimated 4 million people in the US who work as drivers. With some studies suggesting full automation will reduce employment in this sector by two-thirds,[6] Tom's worry about his job seems reasonable.

Many others, like Tom, are becoming aware of the impact of robots on their job. The word 'robot' was first introduced in Karel Capek's 1920 science fiction play *R.U.R.* The origins are from the Czech word *robota* – meaning forced labour or drudgery. Consistent with this original definition, robots are adept at taking on repetitive and dull tasks. Today more than 2 million robots operate around the world, mostly in manufacturing, with the highest concentration in South Korea where there are fifty robots for every thousand people. This concentration will rise even further with entrepreneur Elon Musk anticipating 'the alien dreadnought' factory, a production line with no people. As he explains, 'you can't have people in the production line, otherwise you drop to people speed'.[7]

Improvements in the technological quality of robots and further declines in their price will inevitably lead to robots replacing workers beyond the manufacturing sector. In the service sector you may already have met 'Pepper', the diminutive childlike machines that Softbank introduced in 2014 in its Tokyo branches. Across the city, Pepper is used as a receptionist or greeter in a range of banks and offices, welcoming customers and providing basic information about services. The robot reduces employment costs and frees up the sales team to have longer and more focused conversations with their customers.

The range of possible service-sector applications is vast. Henn-na hotel in Japan describes itself as a robot hotel, with a head robot chef (Andrew) that specialises in making *okonomiyaki* (Japanese omelette) and others which check guests into the hotel and help with their luggage.[8] Meanwhile in California, 'Sally' is a robot that makes salads; 'Flippy' is a robot that flips burgers; 'Botlr' works in hotels providing extra towels and toiletries; while Italian firm Makr Shakr is developing a robot bartender. Technology's ceaseless march to solve humanity's problems even led Domino's in 2016 to provide the first drone-delivered pizza in New Zealand – a peri-peri chicken and cranberry pizza delivered to a couple in Whangaparaoa, New Zealand.

You can certainly expect to be served by a robot – will you also be cared for by one?[9] By 2030 the likelihood is that you will, and in countries such as Japan, with declining and aging populations, robots will provide that extra pair of hands that family and friends can't. You can also expect to find robots in your home, taking care of basic tasks like vacuuming, paying bills, and automatically ordering your daily needs from food to medicine.

What qualifications will be needed to safeguard careers?

For much of history, human ingenuity created tools that augmented and substituted *physical power* – the stone axe, the wheel, the spinning jenny. Using machines that augment or substitute *intellectual power* is altogether more revolutionary and harder to understand. Advances in Artificial Intelligence are bringing technology into a cognitive arena which traditionally has been the preserve of humans.

Smart machines have of course been around for a while. In 1979, VisiCalc was launched: this was the first fully working version of the now ubiquitous computer spreadsheet. It replaced literal spreadsheets – large 11 inch by 17 inch sheets of paper on which a clerk added rows and columns of numbers, a time-intensive process subject to human error. Much has changed since 1979: crucially, the current generation of smart machines make their own calculations in order to achieve set goals, as opposed to following predefined rules to perform specific tasks.

Enabling this goal-directed breakthrough has been machine learning (ML), which rather than a sequential form ('if – then') of calculation uses algorithms, usually a neural network.[10] This means machines can compute their own understanding of a problem and adapt to changing circumstances. In doing so, AI mimics some of the operations of the human brain – but does so more quickly. This shift to ML makes full use of the quartet of laws which together enable the fast transmission and processing of vast amounts of information.

Consider the AlphaGo program that in 2017 defeated Lee Sedol, the eighteen-time 'Go' world champion. AlphaGo was created by DeepMind, a British AI company acquired by Google in 2014. Three different versions of AlphaGo were created: Lee,

15

Master and Zero.[11] The Lee and Master versions were, to different degrees, trained by being provided with the rules of the game, knowledge of past matches, human guidance and instructions provided by experts. Zero, by contrast, was simply given the rules of the game and instructed to play the game a large number of times itself, thereby devising its own playing strategies. In other words, AlphaGo Zero was its own teacher. Over forty days, AlphaGo Zero played 29 million games, building up a database unrivalled by any human player. Within four days it was outperforming AlphaGo Lee; within thirty-four days, it was beating AlphaGo Master.

What's fascinating is that AlphaGo Zero was able to develop strategies that were qualitatively different to those used when humans play. As the creators wrote: 'In the space of a few days, starting *tabula rasa,* AlphaGo Zero was able to rediscover much of this Go knowledge, as well as novel strategies that provide new insights into the oldest of games.'

While VisiCalc was programmed to quickly and reliably perform complex calculations, AlphaGo instead was instructed to achieve a goal – win the game. It uses in some sense judgement and intention to effect outcomes beyond human capability.

It is this combination of ability and intent, replacement and augmentation that means, regardless of whether you are a cashier, a truck driver, a lawyer or a financial advisor, the nature of your job will change profoundly. With that, of course, comes the risk of job losses – with spreadsheets came the loss of around 400,000 bookkeeping jobs.[12]

Ying is an accountant in Sydney and is experiencing this first-hand. Her firm's investment in AI brought a dramatic reduction in employees needed in the account-processing department, which Ying managed. Her plan had been to work until she retired at sixty-five, but now at fifty-five she has been told to find another job in the next six months. Ying feels she is well qualified with a bachelor's degree in accounting and a postgraduate qualification as a chartered accountant, but despite making several job applications she hasn't been asked for a single interview. Previously it has been those with less education who have been most impacted by technology but Ying, even with her professional qualifications, is struggling.

Estelle works as a cashier in a London supermarket and is facing similar problems to Ying. As ever more customers use the self-service checkout, the time doesn't seem far away when her own store will copy the Amazon Go convenience stores and introduce a no cashier policy. That worries her as she receives a limited financial contribution from her ex-husband, who has already lost his warehouse job to automation. To supplement her income, Estelle is working night shifts in the local nursing home. Her friends have suggested that she work there full-time, but that role requires a qualification that takes two years. She has already dropped out of two evening courses and feels she has neither the time nor the money to go down that route.

Ying and Estelle show the breadth of the educational challenge society faces as technology and longevity combine forces. Educational institutions will need to evolve and provide new courses and support to help them with such challenges. Governments too will have to extend their involvement in education to support lifelong learning.

In which areas will humans outperform machines?

If the quartet of laws continues, then future technologies will make AlphaGo seem as limited and unexciting as VisiCalc does to us today. Whilst current machines are smart at performing particular tasks such as chess, Go, and poker, they are not really intelligent in a way a human is.[13] Human brains are incredibly well adapted to asking and framing questions, posing hypotheses, switching between a variety of different problems, and imagining future possibilities. With this in mind, the ultimate goal is General AI (AGI) – machines that can successfully achieve any intellectual task a human can. The breakthrough moment for AGI will be achieving 'the singularity' – this is the point when machines are capable of inventing machines smarter than themselves, leading to an inevitable rapid development cycle until these machines become vastly more capable than humans in all dimensions.

In contemplating this future, it's important to make a distinction between AI and AGI. Many of the bleakest views – economically, socially and existentially – are informed by potential developments in AGI, which suggest an unnerving world where machines are better at everything than humans. However, research is currently far from this point and even fairly basic tests, like identifying road signs in pictures that CAPTCHA[14] demands, outwits most AI. Exactly when or even if AGI will emerge is subject to much debate. MIT's Max Tegmark quotes a survey of computer scientists whose estimates range from between a few years to never.[15] The average estimate is that AGI will be developed by 2055 – within the possible lifetime of anyone currently below the age of sixty. But until the advent of AGI, humans will have advantages over machines.

As AI advances, the type of skills and jobs where humans outperform machines will inevitably change. Hans Moravec of the Robotics Institute, Carnegie Mellon University, visualises this with a metaphor of the 'landscape of human competence'. Imagine a map of islands and sea with the contours of the map representing human competence. The higher the elevation of a peak, the more pronounced is human competence. Now imagine the current sea level represents the tasks AI can already perform. Over time, the sea level rises and ever more areas of human competence are lost to the surging tide of AI proficiency.

Those human competences that are already submerged include arithmetical calculations in spreadsheets, pattern recognition and playing chess and Go. The water level is currently lapping on the shores of the human competencies of translation, investment decisions, speech recognition and driving. By the time you read this book these areas may already be under water.

The areas of human competence first conceded to machines are those involving routine and programmatic tasks. The higher, more impregnable peaks include more 'human' qualities, such as social interaction, caring and empathy, management and leadership, creation and innovation. In the face of this, each of us has to head to high ground in order to avoid the expanding reach of AI as it submerges more of the landscape of human competence.

Even if AGI does eventually arrive, it will be these higher peaks that will provide humans with a comparative even if not absolute advantage over machines.

All this points to a dynamic and changing landscape of jobs and careers in the decades ahead. Hiroki's father worked in the same firm for his whole career, but Hiroki, in his early twenties, cannot envisage that for himself. Given the power of new technologies it is unlikely that a single job skill will suffice, and as technology transforms the corporate landscape, he cannot imagine any company he joins now will last a lifetime.

These extraordinary technologies aren't just changing jobs, they are also changing how we work. Radhika lives and works in Mumbai; she is part of a global gig economy where, as a freelancer, she provides her services for firms around the world who pay her for performing specific tasks. Radhika has never worked for a traditional employer and as a freelancer has to actively look for her next project. She might have autonomy and freedom, but she has none of the development, promotion or training opportunities her friends in traditional work experience. Radhika and Hiroki are both asking themselves how they design and construct their career in a world where traditional jobs and long-term relationships with an employer are disappearing.

ENABLING LONGER LIVES

These immediate concerns of Radhika and Hiroki about the impact of technology on their work and their careers are only part of the challenges they face. Another outcome of human ingenuity – longevity – is likely to play an even larger role in shaping their future lives.

For whilst human ingenuity is creating extraordinary technologies, it has also substantially increased life expectancy and in doing so has brought into question basic assumptions about life-span and life stages. In many countries human ingenuity is enabling many over the age of sixty-five to live healthy lives, and this has led to further questioning and confusion around the process of aging and our assumptions about an aging society and what it means to be old.

The oldest person to have lived, or at least that can be officially documented, was Jeanne Calment, who died in 1997 at the age of 122 years and 164 days in France. In 1965, at the age of ninety, she famously signed a contract with her lawyer, André-François Raffray, that would see him pay her a monthly sum of 2,500 francs so that upon her death, he would own her apartment. Raffray died aged seventy-seven in 1995 when Calment was still 'only' 120. He ended up paying more than double what Calment's apartment was worth. In the words of Calment, 'in life, one sometimes makes bad deals'.

Jeanne Calment is exceptional. At the time of writing, the oldest person alive is Kane Tanaka from Japan, who is 116 years and 301 days old. However, while such 'superagers' are unusual, in the last 150 years there has been a continual increase in 'best practice life expectancy', which is defined by the country at any moment in time that has the highest *average* life expectancy at birth. Currently best practice life expectancy is defined by Japanese women, who have a life expectancy of eighty-seven.[16]

For more than a century, best practice life expectancy has been increasing at a remarkable rate of two to three years every decade.[17] This implies that, on average, each generation is living six to nine years longer than the previous generation. As a consequence, a twenty-year-old American man today has a greater chance of having a living *grand*mother than a twenty-year-old American man in 1900 had of having a living *mother*.

If this trend continues, then children born today in the developed world have a more than 50 per cent chance of living past a hundred. Even if the rate of increase halves, children born today still have a greater than 30 per cent chance of making it to a hundred. As a result of this, the number of people aged over one hundred is the fastest-growing demographic group across the world.

Madoka is in her twenties and as a Japanese woman is one of those who define best practice life expectancy. Whilst life expectancy in the UK and US has in recent years been declining,[18] in

Japan it continues to rise. Between 2010 and 2016, life expectancy for Japanese women aged sixty-five increased at a rate of eight weeks a year, roughly 1.5 years a decade.

Madoka lives in one of the most developed countries of the world – what can Radhika, living in India, expect? She doesn't yet have the same chance of reaching a hundred but developing countries like India are experiencing even more dramatic *increases* in life expectancy as they catch up with the richest countries. So Radhika can expect to live a great deal longer than her parents. In India (and China) over the last fifty years, life expectancy has increased by twenty-six (and twenty-four) years. That's a much faster *rate* of increase than in rich countries – equivalent to five years in every decade. The life choices that Radhika's parents made offer little guidance to Radhika given how much longer she can expect to live. Madoka and Radhika will have to do, something that neither their parents or grandparents ever had to do namely to try and structure and finance for a potential hundred-year life.

How can we stay fit, healthy, active and engaged for longer?

Radhika and Madoka welcome these gains in life expectancy but they want to live these added years in good health. At seventy-one, Clive is much fitter and healthier than his parents were at that age and is looking forward to many more years of life. Yet whilst some of his older friends are in good health, others are struggling. He is wondering how to spend his retirement to maximise his chances of remaining in good health.

In most countries, the good news is that the majority of these years of extra life are healthy. Broadly, the proportion of life spent in good health has remained at least constant as life expectancy has improved,[19] and in many countries it has increased. For example, in the UK between 2000–14, life expectancy increased by 3.5 years, of which 2.8 years were healthy (on a self-reported basis). Looking forward, a UK study estimates that by the year 2035, more than 80 per cent of those aged 65–74 will be living free of chronic conditions (today it's 69 per cent).[20] More than half (58 per cent) of those aged 75–84 can expect to do the same

21

(today it's 50 per cent). This improvement in how we age means that these extra years of life have not been inserted at the end of life, simply extending a period of frailty. Rather it is as if late middle age and early old age has been extended instead.

The challenge is that as people live longer, they tend to suffer more from non-communicable diseases, such as Alzheimer's, cancers, respiratory problems and diabetes. They are also more likely to experience these simultaneously, leading to a rise in 'co-morbidities'. It is important though to distinguish between two distinct effects. If we compare a fifty-year-old and an eighty-year-old, the older person is more likely to suffer from non-communicable diseases and co-morbidities; but over time, because people are aging better, an eighty-year-old today is less likely than an eighty-year-old twenty years ago to suffer ill health.

Should Madoka and Radhika plan for an even longer life than Clive and their parents? In the debate about technological innovations and the likely continuation of Moore's Law, there are arguments that past trends can't be expected to continue into the future. The same debate is taking place for those who study longevity. Some experts believe life expectancy has reached a limit and may now even fall as diabetes, obesity and rising resistance to antibiotics take their toll. Others point out that whilst evolution has helped remove many genetic abnormalities, it has never really had an influence on old age as this occurs after humans are reproductive. This matters because, if gains in best practice life expectancy are to continue at their historical rate, it will require an acceleration in the rate of improvement of the survival chances of older people.

However, even under these pessimistic assumptions, many children born today can reasonably expect to live into their nineties.[21] And the higher their income and education and the healthier their lifestyle, the greater their probable lifespan.

And whilst some believe life expectancy is plateauing, others argue there is much more to come. It is interesting that whilst futurists tend to overpredict the pace at which technology will develop, government statisticians have a history of underpredicting life expectancy gains. You can see this in

22

Figure 1.1, which shows forecasts of future male life expectancy produced since 1975 by the UK's Office for National Statistics (ONS), compared with the life expectancy trends actually realised. What is clear is a persistent tendency to underestimate future gains in life expectancy.

A growing group of scientists are becoming ever more optimistic about future life expectancy gains.[22] This optimism arises from a shift in perspective towards seeing many illnesses as a function of aging itself, and this moves the research strategy to understanding why people age.[23] This in turn raises the hope that eventually the aging process can be slowed down, or even potentially reversed. If successful, this research programme could lead to life expectancy increases accelerating in the years ahead. Some of the most optimistic researchers even believe *longevity escape velocity* could be reached: that happens when life expectancy increases by more than a year every year. If this were to occur, humans would be entering the realms of immortality. Lifespans of 500 or 1,000 years are startling, but the most likely immediate pay-off from this research will be improving *health span* by slowing down the rate at which chronic conditions and non-communicable diseases arise. This offers the extraordinary possibility of remaining healthy until the final moments of life.

FIGURE 1.1 Life expectancy projections and out-turns (source: ONS)

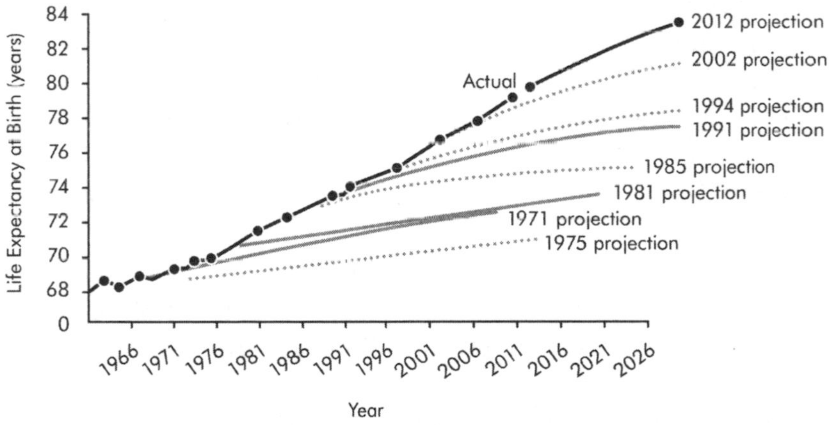

The foundational principle here is that how we age is malleable and not fixed. Historically, osteoporosis and Alzheimer's were considered a normal part of aging but are now classified as diseases by the World Health Organisation. Will the same eventually happen to aging itself? If so, it would be one of the most outstanding displays of human ingenuity in history. There have already been some fascinating results: research has managed to increase the lifespans of worms tenfold,[24] and longevity gains have also been achieved in mice and dogs. The big question is whether these results will carry over into humans.

Although progress is being made, the signs of escape velocity remain some way off. There are obvious challenges to testing treatments on humans, especially as the success can only be known at the very end of life which implies lengthy trials. However, given the growing interest and research in the area, it seems plausible that treatments will be developed that continue to contribute to further increases in health span and potentially lifespan. If best practice life expectancy is to continue to increase at the same rate as the past fifty years, then these scientific breakthroughs will be needed.

What will be the impact of longevity on families and communities?

Madoka in Japan and Radhika in India can expect to live longer than their parents, and a great deal longer than their grandparents. As the same happens to millions of other people at the *aggregate* level this is having profound implications on populations of people, the choices they make and the structure of the societies they live in.

In the Indian village where Radhika was born, the average family had six children – Radhika has four brothers and one sister. In this rural community children were viewed as an asset – both in terms of their labour and their capacity to support aging parents. Radhika in her late twenties has an entirely different view of children. Like many other young Indian women, she is better educated than her mother's generation and is pursuing a career. Considering the cost of raising a family, she sees children as an economic liability.

As others make the same choice, fertility rates around the world are falling. This choice is profoundly influenced by the education level of women. Demographers have developed a rule of thumb: on average a woman with no formal education has more than six children; if she has finished primary education she is likely to have four children, and if she has finished secondary school then the likelihood is that she will have no more than two children. As more women around the world are educated, the UN predicts that by the end of the century the average global family will have two children compared to two and a half today.

Radhika and Madoka are therefore both looking at a very different life course from their parents – they are likely to live longer than their parents and also have fewer children. This is the basis of their questioning of family roles and responsibilities and their desire to establish their own career and working identity.

Across whole populations, these demographic trends are having, and will continue to have, a profound impact. As demographers such as Oxford University's Sarah Harper have noted,[25] when countries develop economically, they experience a 'demographic transition' – a period when both fertility rates and mortality rates fall. Society therefore moves from a period when lots of children are born each year and lots of people die, to a period when fewer children per family are born and ever more people survive into old age.

The consequence of this demographic transition is that older population cohorts increase in size relative to younger cohorts, and so the average age of society increases. We can see this playing out across the world: in 1950 the average age was twenty-four; by 2017 it had risen to thirty; and is expected to be thirty-six by the year 2050.

The pace of this demographic transition reflects the speed and breadth of economic growth in a country. Higher income leads to better nutrition, education and health care along with higher wages, all of which contribute to lower birth rates and longer lives. Madoka's parents in Japan experienced the economic boom that followed the Second World War when, from 1955 until 1972, the average economic growth rate of the country was 9 per cent per annum. This made for a rapid demographic transition as the birth rate fell and longevity increased. Other countries, such as China, that have recently undergone rapid economic growth are also experiencing a similarly sharp demographic transition. In 1950 the average age in China was twenty-four – the global average, but following a period of dramatic GDP growth, by 2017 the average age had risen to thirty-seven (compared to a global average of thirty) and is forecast to reach forty-eight by 2050 (more than a decade older than the predicted global average of thirty-six at that time).[26]

With the demographic transition comes an increase in the proportion of people over the age of sixty-five. Take Clive who was born in 1948 – of his age cohort in the UK, nearly 80 per cent celebrated their seventieth birthday. Never before have so many survived so long. Contrast that with Clive's parents: in their age cohort, less than half lived to seventy. Indeed, the UK government predicts that almost all (90 per cent) of Clive's grandchildren's generation will live to see the age of seventy.

The impact is felt across the world. As Figure 1.2 shows, for the first time in human history today there are more people alive over the age of sixty-five than under the age of five.

From now until the year 2050 in every country in the world, more of the share of the population will be over sixty-five. Currently it is 1 in 12 and by 2050 it will be 1 in 6. This is not just a rich country issue. Today there are twice as many people aged over sixty in developing countries as there are in the developed world. By 2030 there will be three times more, and by 2050 four times more. And as we described in the Introduction, in China estimates suggest that by 2050 there will be more than 438 million people aged over sixty-five, that's more people than the current US population.

It's not just the over-65s who are increasing in number – there is also dramatic growth expected in the over-80s. Currently around

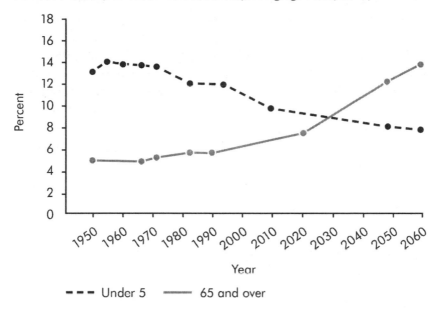

the world, 126 million people are over the age of eighty; by the year 2050 this is estimated to reach 447 million. The increase is most dramatic in Japan, with the proportion of the population aged over eighty expected to rise from 8 per cent today to 18 per cent by 2050.

These demographic shifts are also having an effect not just on the structure of the population but also its size. Whether a population is growing, static or even declining depends on the stage of the country's demographic transition. Many African countries are at an early stage of the transition where mortality rates are falling faster than the birth rate and so the population is increasing. Take Nigeria, which in 1950 had a population of 38 million. By 2017 this had grown to 186 million with half of the population under the age of fifteen, and only 3 per cent over the age of sixty-five.

As countries move through the demographic transition the birth rate declines to a similar level as the mortality rate and population growth begins to slow. In some cases, where the birth rate goes below the mortality rate, more people are dying than being born and so the population starts to decline. In 1950 there wasn't a single country at this stage – between now and 2050 it is estimated that more than fifty countries will see population decline.

In Japan and China, where the fall in fertility has been very pronounced, the population size has and will decline dramatically. Madoka knows this already, she reads constantly in the press about the shrinking Japanese population – from a high in 2004 of 128 million, to an expected 109 million by 2050, declining to 84.5 million by 2100. When Ying talks to her relatives in China, they are also aware of this. Currently the population is 1.36 billion; forecasts suggest that by 2050 it will have declined to 1 billion people.

How can everyone remain economically productive and work for longer?

Madoka worries about what this will mean for the economy too. All things being equal, for every 1 per cent fall in population, there is a 1 per cent fall in GDP growth. So if in Japan the population declines to 88 million by 2065, this would result in a decline of 30 per cent from its current value. This means that over the next fifty years, GDP growth will be lowered by around 0.6 per cent per annum. Across the world this issue is rising up the agenda, leading governments to ask what can be done to support economic growth in the face of an aging and declining population?

As government and individuals wrestle with the implications of longer lives, there are three areas that urgently need social ingenuity: the financing of pensions; the provision of health care; and achieving equity between the multiple generations now living together.

On the face of it the finances of an aging society make grim reading. If across a population the majority of people retire at sixty-five or earlier, then as the proportion of people aged over sixty-five increases so we can expect economic growth to slow. In the European Union over the next forty years the expectation is that the population of people of working age (or more accurately those under the age of sixty-five) will fall by 20 per cent. This decline in the number of workers will mean a reduction in annual GDP growth (on a per capita basis) of 0.5 per cent (20/40). Given that per capita growth has been at just 0.7 per cent over the past decade, that's a worrying trend for governments.

The fear of slower economic growth combined with the certainty of a rising number of people aged over sixty-five is placing considerable pressure on both government and private pension schemes. This is where social ingenuity will be so crucial – in terms of how long people work, the assumptions of what aging is, and the willingness of corporations to drop deeply embedded negative stereotypes about the performance and motivation of the over-60s.

Consider a great example of past social ingenuity – the creation of state pensions. These were introduced in Bismarck's Germany in 1889 and subsequently adopted by many other countries – the UK in 1908 and the US in 1935. Their introduction meant people could avoid spending their final years working, living in extreme poverty or dependent on the (often resentful) support of their children. The change has been dramatic: in the UK today, a smaller proportion of pensioners live in poverty than for the working population as a whole.[27]

When these first pensions were introduced in the UK, the pensionable age was set at seventy, at a time when median life expectancy for those born in 1838 (who would be seventy in 1908) was forty-five. The result was that only a small proportion of people qualified, not many lived long enough to receive a pension, and those that did tended not to live for very long. For governments, financing these pensions was relatively easy.

Since that time the parameters have changed considerably. Take Clive. Most of his cohort have reached state pension age (which had been reduced from seventy to sixty-five) and are expected to live a lot longer than past generations. The impact on government finances is clear: in 1970 pension costs across the OECD (Organisation for Economic Co-operation and Development) were around 4 per cent of GDP, by 2017 they had risen to 8 per cent and is expected to rise to almost 10 per cent by 2050. It is no surprise that governments are acting by raising the pension age and reducing the generosity of pensions.

In his forties, Tom is beginning to worry about his savings and retirement plans. He is a member of the Teamsters Union whose pension fund is under pressure due to a rising number of retirees, stock market falls during the financial crisis and the bankruptcy of a number of trucking companies. The result has been a cut in pension benefits of around 29 per cent. Tom is beginning to realise he will have to work for longer than he expected in order to finance the lifestyle he wants in retirement. In *The 100-Year Life* we calculated that someone of Tom's age will probably have to work into their early seventies in order to finance their pension; for Madoka, now in her twenties, her working life may even stretch into her eighties.

This means that Tom in his forties and Ying in her mid-fifties face the prospect of another thirty and twenty years of work respectively. That's forcing them to really consider how they can become social pioneers, whilst also putting pressure on governments, educators and corporations to be more innovative in their attitudes and practices. That is crucial because far from supporting longer working careers, many current government and corporate policies and practices place barriers in the way of remaining productive for longer.

When Clive looks back and thinks of his grandmother, his assumption was that she was 'old' at seventy. But when he thinks about himself at seventy, he doesn't feel the same way. As more people live healthily into their eighties and nineties, the traditional definition of 'old' as over sixty-five is proving to be too broad. Clive struggles against ageist assumptions about what he is capable of doing at his age and what he should be doing. When governments and corporations assume that those over sixty-five are 'old', 'dependent' and 'unproductive', then this inevitably leads to economic and social problems.

That is why it is so crucial that our social ingenuity is focused on reinventing careers in midlife and reshaping corporate policy to support and enable people to work into their seventies and eighties.

*How can health systems be created that focus
on healthy aging?*

As well as rising concerns around pensions, there is also growing
anxiety about health costs. A glance at Figure 1.3 makes this clear
and shows why social ingenuity is so desperately needed. The
data from the OECD countries reveals the extent to which the
cost of health care increases with age. It demonstrates the sharp
rise from the late sixties age group onwards. Indeed in some
countries, such as the Netherlands, the health costs for the over-
80s are as high as two-thirds of the average income. As the population ages, more of society's resources will be needed to provide
health care for the old, assuming no change in citizens' health or
in how health care is provided.

As the population ages, the disease burden shifts from infectious diseases to the diseases of the old. This has important cost
implications because, whilst death from infectious diseases tends to
be fast, dying from non-communicable diseases tends to be a much
longer process and is expensive to treat. Take the case of Alzheimer's,

Figure 1.3 Per capita health spending by age group as a share of GDP per
capita, 2011 (source: OECD *Health Statistics*)

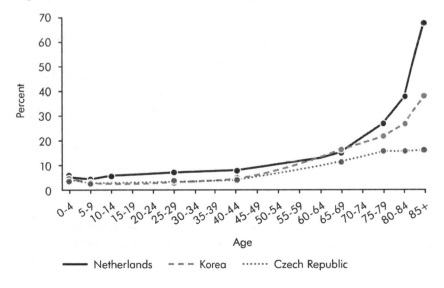

which currently has no cure or effective treatment and where medical costs are high. The American Alzheimer's Association estimates costs of around $287,000 per person per year in 2010, compared to $175,000 for heart disease and $173,000 for cancer.

This shift from infectious diseases to non-communicable diseases has important implications for cost – it also has important implications for health care strategies. That is because there is growing evidence that non-communicable diseases are significantly influenced by lifestyle. So here the challenge for social ingenuity is to find ways to support people to keep mentally and physically active. For governments this means a crucial shift towards preventative health care, whilst for individuals it raises profound questions about how to live life so as to age as healthily and happily as possible.

How can constructive intergenerational relationships be forged?

Hiroki is in his early twenties and both his parents are alive, as are all four of his grandparents. Whenever his family gathers together, he and his cousins feel both young and outnumbered. Compared to past generations, Hiroki has fewer siblings, fewer cousins and so family gatherings are less dominated by the young. Hiroki and Madoka are very mindful that although they may have fewer children than their parents, they will have substantial obligations to older relatives.

The obligation that Madoka and Hiroki feel to their family is reflected at the society level in terms of the possibility of intergenerational conflict. Government policy around the world is changing to accommodate longer lives: retirement dates are being pushed back, pensions reduced, and taxes increased. But, from an intergenerational perspective the worry is that whilst the younger generation are paying higher taxes to finance the pensions of the old, they will have less generous pensions for themselves. One UK study estimates that over their lifetime, future generations will be worse off by nearly a £100,000 in terms of lower benefits or higher taxes.[28] All this is occurring at the same time as economic growth seems to be slowing compared to that which their parents experienced.

Concerns about intergenerational equity are not restricted to public finances: the young will also inevitably experience more transitions and work for longer. They may also find that a university qualification will not be a sufficient entry to a professional job. In some subjects, the graduate wage premium is becoming non-existent.

As technology and longevity change the fundamentals of how we live and work, social ingenuity will be crucial to find ways to make good the promises made to past generations, while also offering progress and opportunity to the young. We have to ensure that the young and old equitably share the burdens and opportunities of longer lives.

HUMAN SOLUTIONS TO HUMAN QUESTIONS

Human ingenuity has led to extraordinary new technologies and substantial gains in healthy life expectancy. Yet it is clear to us that the answers to the question we have posed will be solved through *social ingenuity.*

For whilst these inventions hold the potential to improve people's lives, unlocking this potential will require deep-seated changes – in how lives are structured and in how educational, corporate and governmental institutions redefine the context within which we live.

The questions we have raised do not relate to a science-fiction world. They are about the world we live in today, and the world we and our children will live in over the coming decades. They are not metaphysical concerns about the future of humanity – rather, they address the very real and practical issues about how each of us should conduct our lives.

The agenda is profound. If we are to flourish as humans, we must focus our extraordinary human ingenuity on inventing a new life course and reimagining our social norms, practices and institutions.

2

HUMAN FLOURISHING

How can we capitalise on our extraordinary human ingenuity and invent a new long life?

Our most unique human skills are imagining future possible outcomes and arriving at solutions to complex and difficult questions. With smarter machines and more years of healthy life ahead of us, we now have a great opportunity to engage these unique human skills to imagine and express more fully our human potential.

In answering the questions we posed earlier, what is certain is that many of the old assumptions that anchored life choices and actions look increasingly misplaced or even wrong. Ying assumed that she would be in her job until retirement and she would be financially secure; Tom assumed that his trucking job would last for long enough for him to qualify for what he thought was a healthy Teamster pension; Hiroki and Madoka's parents assumed their children would want the lives they led; Clive assumed he would be happy with a leisurely retirement.

Yet without these anchors, we are in a sense unmoored. We are in a place between the certainties of the past and the ambiguity of the future. You may have first-hand experience of being unmoored – perhaps as a result of emigrating, a significant career move, or a change in family circumstances such as divorce. During this period of transition your identity is no longer *what it was,* and *what it could be* is not yet clear. You have not yet adapted to the new country, or the new job, or your new marital status.

Anthropologists call this period of betwixt and between *liminality*. Arnold van Gennep, in his studies of the rites of passage, observed how, as the certainties of the past begin to fade, people feel they are losing their footing.[1] If you are sensing this feeling of loose footing you are not alone: families, communities, the workplace and whole populations are also experiencing it in response to the changes brought about by technology and longevity.

Whilst the anxiety associated with making a transition and experimenting will always be present, this is where social ingenuity must play a role. For each of us that means looking forward, building insight, facing truths and unflinchingly looking at what is and what could be – in other words becoming a *social pioneer*.

In reality this is difficult because as we look forward and build insight, we cannot know for sure what the future will bring. So against this backdrop of uncertainty, being *curious* becomes ever more important. This is clear from the psychological studies of Harvard Business School's Francesca Gino. In her research she identifies the crucial role that curiosity plays in helping people adapt more quickly when they are faced with uncertainty and external pressure. Those who are curious arrive more easily at creative solutions and, importantly, are less likely to fall prey to stereotypes and wrong assumptions.

Tom has some of the curiosity of a social pioneer. He is keeping abreast of developments in autonomous vehicles by reading and looking closely at the updates his union send him. He is also reaching into his network to talk to fellow drivers about what they are experiencing. Looking back, Ying wished she'd exercised some of this same curiosity. Instead she is now reacting to the loss of her job with very little in the way of preparation.

Whilst important, being a social pioneer requires more though than being curious, thinking forward and imagining. Crucially it also means having the determination and courage to take action. In the face of new technologies and longer lives, the way we currently work, our career paths, education and relationship structures are looking increasingly unsustainable. And that means we have to start behaving differently. For some people taking action will mean following in the footsteps of social innovators; for others it will mean being the courageous trailblazer – no longer relying on past social norms or existing institutions to guide or support.

People of all ages are already acting as social pioneers. They are expanding their insight by forging new networks of friends and acquaintances; they are experimenting with their roles and responsibilities at home; they are creating projects and building new ways of living and working. This is not an easy task, and there will be times when it is simpler to maintain the status quo. Ying now realises she worked so hard to maintain the status quo of her career path that she failed to anticipate or prepare for a major transition.

THE REDESIGN OF LIFE

If the challenge is nothing less than redesigning how we live our lives, what should be the principles that underpin this redesign?

Clearly economic considerations will be central to any redesign – a foundational principle has to be securing a 'good life'. It is economic fears which underpin worries that robots will eradicate all human jobs, and that society cannot afford long retirements amidst the growing proportion of older people. So a crucial response to longevity and technology must be securing a good standard of living.

History certainly provides grounds for optimism. For whilst during previous technological transitions there may have been winners and losers, in the long run technology has brought about spectacular improvements in the standard of living. For most of human history the average world citizen had a lifestyle based on an annual income of around $90 to $150, expressed in 1990 prices. Starting in the eighteenth century, living standards began to improve, reaching $200 by 1800; $700 by 1900, and more than $6,500 by the year 2000.[2] There is every reason to believe the same can happen again in the wake of current developments.

We also now work less: in 1870 the average French working week was sixty-six hours;[3] it is now thirty-six hours. Further, since the introduction of retirement people now take extra leisure in the later stages of life. Looking forward, smart new technologies have the potential to make further reductions to domestic hours and offer the prospect of a four-day working week.

These innovations all reflect averages, but for humans to flourish *everyone* has to gain from technological advances and longer lives. Concern about inequality isn't just about individual outcomes but also, as Princeton historian Walter Scheidel argues, about social risk. His view is that, across human history, increases in inequality are only ever reduced by war, revolution or catastrophe.[4]

That is a concern because not only has inequality in both income and life expectancy been rising in many countries over recent decades, but future trends suggest it is likely to continue. When the longevity gap between the top and bottom 1 per cent of the US population in terms of income is fifteen years for men and ten for women,[5] no wonder these issues are rising up the political agenda.

Just as individually we need to restructure our life course, so too our institutions and policies that provide social insurance and support to those with few resources or who experience economic misfortune need to change. Ying has the economic resources to make the transition she is now faced with, but Estelle will struggle to do so. A wide range of policies will be needed to ensure that everyone benefits from this ongoing and long-lasting transition.

Human flourishing

It is impossible to argue against the principle that humans want more rather than fewer resources; prefer less to more work; and would rather feel economically safe than insecure. Our response to technology and longevity must have achieving economic prosperity at its core. But the real beating heart of the human agenda has to be more ambitious.

Think of it this way: if humans were simply to become the pets of super-intelligent robots, they would have plentiful resources, leisure and safety. But this is not a life humans aspire to – we humans look to the future and have hopes, ambitions and dreams; we have human capabilities that need to be fulfilled; we seek not just to prosper but to attain a sense of belonging and esteem – of meaningful identity.

The principles that shape social ingenuity must therefore ensure *both* a good standard of living and that we flourish as humans. The touchstones of a good standard of living are well understood – but what of flourishing?

Our focus will be on three central touchstones: each reflects deeply held human characteristics, while also providing a helpful way of addressing the questions we have raised.

> **Narrate**: navigating a life story and creating a narrative that brings meaning to life and helps navigate the choices we face.
> *What will my job be? What skills will I need? What does a career look like? What does it mean to be 'old'?*

> **Explore**: learning and transforming in ways that enable us to successfully make the transitions that will be part of our life.
> *How do I explore the new career options that a longer future provides? How will I learn the new skills they require? How do I experiment with change and navigate through a life of more transitions at new stages?*

> **Relate**: connecting deeply and building and sustaining meaningful relationships.
> *How should I respond to changing family structures? What will a world with fewer children and more old people look like? What can I and others do to achieve intergenerational harmony?*

Narrate: navigating my life story

As children we found stories compelling – they helped us imagine and understand our world and provide a sense of belonging. As we grow into adulthood, these narratives become more focused on issues of identity. This sense of identity – of who we are is located in time – what was, what is now, and what could be. Looking back, we know what was; looking forward we are presented with, as Stanford social psychologists Hazel Markus and Paula Nunus describe, an array of future 'possible selves'.[6] Exploring these 'possible selves' will be key to navigating a life story.

Traditionally the structure was a three-stage life. This took a simple form: full-time education followed by full-time work and then full-time retirement. And because everyone was in lockstep with each other and making transitions at the same time, peer pressure was a significant navigational force.

Many of the framings of this narrative and the nature of these navigational forces are now shifting. Longevity means on average the span of life is *longer*, whilst the disruption of technology creates more frequent *transitions*. It is this combination of lengthening horizons and shortening intervals which will lead inevitably to a new narrative – a *multistage*, rather than a three-stage, life. This shift will profoundly change the answers to the questions we have posed: what a job is, how we work, the way we fashion a career, what it means to age.

As Radhika looks ahead, she is intensely aware of the need to create a unique narrative for her life that could well be very different from her parents'. She wants to be more creative about how she imagines her identity and life story. With a long life ahead of her, she realises she needs to be more thoughtful about the choices she makes, and more aware of the trade-offs she faces between the present and the future, and between time and money.

Explore: learning and transforming

The history of humans is a tale of exploration. Humans have always had a desire to explore the unknown and our sense of exploration runs deeper than geography; it also feeds into a fundamental curiosity in learning about the world.

Neuroscientists such as Jaak Panksepp[7] have discovered there is a physiological part of the brain they term the 'seeking system'. In their neurological experiments they have found this 'seeking system' is activated, in a sense it 'lights up', when the individual engages with novel information or a puzzling task. They also have clear evidence that this neurological stimulation is highly motivating – as London Business School's Daniel Cable shows, we humans delight in exploring.[8]

It seems we all are hard-wired to learn and transform. In the decades ahead, fascinating questions will emerge for us to grapple with as social pioneers. And the increased frequency of transitions will demand that we explore and learn, develop new skills and become comfortable experimenting with new ways of behaving.

Ying is reimagining her life now as she faces up to losing her job. Hers will be a transition where she will have to find new things to do and equip herself with new skills. It will take curiosity and the courage for her to explore her 'possible selves' and the array of options out there. Looking around, she sees few people have taken the route she is imagining – in midlife she is becoming a social pioneer.

Relate: connecting deeply

When George Vaillant directed the longitudinal Harvard study,[9] which explored how people achieve lifetime happiness and satisfaction, one aspect of the research stood out clearly. It is deep, rich and long friendships that have the most positive and profound impact on life outcomes.

Our relationships with others create a sense of belonging and of appreciation. When we are loved and love others, we feel cherished, happy, cared for and understood. When we are not able to relate, we experience rejection and our trust in others is diminished, leaving us feeling lonely, isolated and anxious.

Hiroki and Madoka are wondering how they can develop their own relationship in a way that enables both to have careers, work flexibly and raise a family. They hope their financial and family commitments can be shared equally. Clive is trying to widen his circle of friends. He is beginning to realise how important it is for him to really mix with people who are younger than him – he knows he has much to learn from them and would also like the opportunity to mentor in return.

These deeper relationships capable of negotiation and commitments, and these wider relationship networks all need

41

time to develop. Yet it is clear that the three-stage life of education, work and retirement that emerged in the twentieth century is ill-suited to support this. A sixty-year working career at the intensity currently expected offers little scope for forming good lifelong friendships or spending quality time with children and parents. Retaining the three-stage narrative in the face of longevity will inevitably lead to us losing touch with our most human needs.

One of the seismic events that revealed the power of AI to transform our lives occurred in 1997, when IBM's 'Deep Blue' beat the world chess champion Garry Kasparov. Kasparov later noted that: 'AI will change every aspect of our daily lives, but it won't change our nature, it will reveal it.'[10]

Adapting our life to reimagine our narrative, identify how we will explore the future, and deepen and embed our relationships is the key to how that human nature will be revealed. Over the course of the next few chapters, we will show you how.

PART TWO

HUMAN INGENUITY

3

NARRATE: NAVIGATING MY LIFE STORY

One of our foundational touchstones for human flourishing is our capacity to create a narrative that provides meaning to our life. Both the sequencing and flow of your narrative will change as longevity and technology create more transitions. In navigating life under these conditions, we are faced with some crucial questions: What will my job be? What skills will I need? What does a career look like? What does it mean to be 'old'?

You can think about navigating your own life using the schema presented in Figure 3.1. This shows your life spread out in front of you – the past, present and future. The past is known, so that's depicted as a single path arriving at the present. In the future there is no single known path, but many possible ones (shown as dotted lines), each leading to its own unique set of possible selves.

As you imagine your future life some, but not all, future selves are attainable. Looking at the schema, there is a possible self 'A' that has no obvious route to it. That's because your future options are defined in part by the *platform* upon which your narrative currently rests. A platform comprises your current abilities, health, education attainments, financial circumstances, the state of your personal relationships, and the extent and depth of your networks. This platform is impacted by your past decisions and the events you have experienced. Your future path will shape future platforms, which will in turn determine the choices available to you.

Figure 3.1 Your 'possible selves'

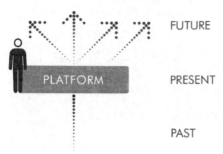

FUTURE

PRESENT

PAST

REIMAGINING AGE

The natural rhythm and structure of your life narrative is marked by calendar time and the passing of the years. In the face of longevity, if we want to reimagine age then we must first decouple the idea of a simple link between time and age. That requires imagining your age is *malleable* – as you live longer and with a greater chance of good health, then what it means to be forty, sixty or eighty years old will change in profound ways. It is this malleability that underpins the redesign of life stages.

On the face of it, the concept of 'age' seems relatively straightforward; even a small child understands it. Yet in a sense the answer a child gives to the question 'how old are you?' is limited because they are thinking of time measured purely in years. The concept of age can also be biological (the age of your body), sociological (how others treat you) and subjective (how old you feel). We can hear these differing concepts of age in our everyday expressions – 'I am feeling my age today', 'They look good for their age', 'You shouldn't be doing that at your age'.

As age becomes malleable, the link between these different concepts of age begins to shift. By the time the child is sixty her biological age could vary considerably from her chronological age, or how she sees herself may be very different from how others see her. As the link between these different concepts of age is disrupted, so we can no longer rely on specific chronological milestones as the structuring mechanism of our life narrative.

That will not be easy. Chronological age is both the dominant form of measuring age and is the foundation of the three-stage life. It also happens to be reinforced by a plethora of educational, social and government practices and policies: go to college at eighteen, get married in your twenties or early thirties, and retire at sixty-five.

We haven't always relied on chronological age; in fact, even birthday parties are a twentieth-century invention. For most of human history, people didn't actually *know* their date or even year of birth. Chronological age became dominant only as governments began to collect accurate birth records in the nineteenth century.[1] From that point it was chronological age that provided the time structure to our lives.

The result is a form of *numerical determinism*. Social norms and stereotypes, as well as assumptions about our own future life, are pinned down to a number – how many years since you were born? This numerical determinism is both fundamentally misleading and produces the age stereotyping that restricts how people think about their lives and those of others.

What is it to be 'old'?

In the rhythm of your own life's narrative, you will have your own sense of what it is to be young and what it is to be old. Yet as chronological, biological, sociological and subjective age shift in relationship to one another, then what it means to be 'old' changes. This is already apparent in the new words gerontologists are introducing to describe age: 'young-old' (aged 60–69), 'old-old' (70–79) and 'oldest-old' (80+).

But to better understand what it means to be 'old', we must introduce a further measure – *thanatological age*. This defines age not by how long it is since you were born, but rather by how long you have left to live. That is not straightforward because, thankfully, you don't know when you will die. So to get a sense of this we need to look at population statistics and mortality rates (which is the probability of dying at any particular age). At any point in your life, the lower your mortality rate, the less chance you have of dying and the more years you can expect to live.

Thanatological age is therefore negatively correlated with mortality rates. Your mortality rate is also a better proxy of your overall health than your chronological age.[2] Therefore in terms of a population, lower mortality rates are indicative of both better health and having more years left to live – an indicator of being 'younger' in some sense.

To understand these population statistics, consider the case of the UK where in Figure 3.2 we show the average *chronological age* (mean age) since 1950 as well as the average *mortality rate* (shown as mean death rate per 1,000). This shows clearly the difference in measurements of age. Measured chronologically, the population of the UK has never been older. Other things being equal, you would expect this to lead to higher average mortality rates as older people are more likely to die. However, the opposite is occurring – the average mortality rate has *fallen*. Put more simply, despite being older, the average British person has never had so many years left to live. If we focus only on chronological measures of age, it is obvious that the UK is an aging society. But looked at thanatologically, the UK has never been younger.

The explanation lies in the malleability of age – people are living longer and *how* they are aging is changing. As people

FIGURE 3.2 Average age and mortality rate, UK 1950–2017 (source: authors' calculations)

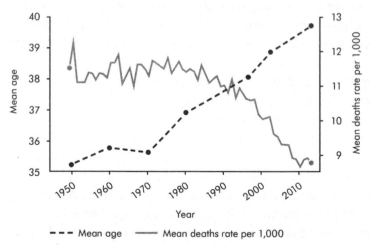

biologically age better, they are healthier and at each age mortality rates fall. This is clear from a study of 21,500 Americans over the age of fifty, which found that biological age (as measured by a range of physical indicators) had fallen relative to chronological age in the period 1988–2010.[3]

The problem of focussing simply on chronological age is that it is a purely *nominal* measure that is unable to take into account what really matters – your health and behaviour. That would be fine if the relationship between health and behaviour at a certain age didn't change, but if age is malleable then using nominal measures becomes confusing.

This confusion is a familiar problem in economics when it comes to inflation. In 1952 a pint of beer cost $0.65 in the US and in 2016 it cost $3.99. It seems obvious that beer has become more expensive over time. However, adjusting for overall inflation, that $0.65 is the equivalent of $5.93 today. In other words, beer is actually cheaper in 2016 than it was in 1952. Similarly, there needs to be an adjustment for *age inflation* – just as each year inflation means that a dollar buys less, so age inflation means that over time a chronological year accounts for less aging.[4]

This has significant implications for what it is to be 'old'. In the UK in 1925 people over the age of sixty-five were entitled to receive a state pension. Today, a seventy-eight-year-old has the same mortality rate as a sixty-five-year-old in 1922. Adjusting for age inflation, the new 'old' is seventy-eight.

The narrative of the 'aging society' is based purely on chronological measures of age, so concludes that there are simply more old people. By not allowing for 'age inflation' it fails to capture the huge changes in how people are aging and ignores the opportunities and solutions that longer lives offer both individually and to society.

Changing your view of your age

It was the US cultural observer Fran Lebowitz who remarked that when she was young, she viewed the old as a different ethnic group, not appreciating the link that time creates between the young and the future old. That is the problem with defining old age by a chronological boundary at sixty-five across which you automatically pass. How you age isn't destiny. It is profoundly influenced by your actions and beliefs.

If you take a chronological approach to your age, then this encourages you to believe aging occurs at the same fixed, invariant rate for everyone – one year, every year. But from the perspective of the malleability of age, this is far from the case. It is fascinating to realise that only a quarter of how you age is genetically determined.[5] That leaves considerable scope for your own actions, as well as events beyond your control, to exert an influence.

That means that what you can do at each age isn't pinned down by the number of candles on your birthday cake. So to exploit the gains of longevity, it is crucial to embrace the idea of the malleability of age. It is also crucial to realise that the implications of your actions are *recursive* – what you do now is connected to and will influence your future. If you think of your life in this recursive way your perspective is more likely to be forward-looking and focus on the time ahead of you rather than the time you have had. That in turn encourages you to make significant investments in your future, learn new skills, build new relationships and invest in your health.

How you frame the malleability of age is driven in part by your subjective sense of aging. An increasing number of studies show that people with positive self-perceptions of aging live, on average, 7.5 years longer than those with negative self-perceptions.[6] A longitudinal study of 6,000 people in the UK aged over fifty reinforced the profound impact of attitudes on how people age.[7] Those who are pessimistic about aging (believing their health will get worse, or they will be lonely) are significantly more likely to have a negative experience of aging.

We each age uniquely, shaped by our behaviours, environment, circumstances and genetics. And as a result of the impact of recursivity, these differences cumulate over time. Over the coming decades as millions more people live into their nineties and beyond, the sheer diversity of aging will become apparent. You will read of amazing athletic achievements of people aged over a hundred, while also knowing people in their forties who lead unadventurous lives, or who are often in poor physical health. Faced with this diversity it is crucial we all shift our narrative away from a simple-minded reliance on chronological measures towards a more individual assessment of your current circumstances and your future needs and aspirations. In other words, to make our own judgement of our biological and subjective age.

Changing your view of the age of others

This change in perspective is not just about how you think about yourself, it's also about how you think of others. This is the essence of 'sociological age', an 'outside in' measure that drives your expectations of others. These social norms about age are important – they create shared agreements and influence stereotypes and behaviour.

Social norms about aging have shifted in the past and will shift again in the future. In England in the 1680s, for example, it was unusual to live to the age of fifty – only about 1 in 5 people achieved this. This was a period when knowledge was not disseminated widely, there were few books and most people could not read. As a consequence, knowledge passed down through the oral traditions of stories and shared experiences. And since older people had accumulated more knowledge, the social norm was that to be over fifty was to be wise. This social perception of age began to shift with the advent of new technologies such as the printing press. Over time, as more books were printed, literacy increased, and the oral traditions of knowledge transfer began to fade. With the fading of oral traditions, the wisdom of the old became less important and as a consequence being over fifty was no longer seen as signifying wisdom.[8]

We are living in a period when the gap between chronological and biological age is changing fast and where social norms are struggling to adapt. In a video produced by the AARP (formerly the American Association of Retired People), young people were asked to do various activities 'just like an old person'.[9] When older people joined them in the video, the gap between the stereo-type and their actual behaviour was striking. In a world where the average age of the Rolling Stones is fifteen years greater than that of the members of the US Supreme Court our social norms need to be updated quickly.

The outdated nature of these existing social norms about age are already causing problems in the labour market. As we will discuss in Chapter 6: The Corporate Agenda, in many companies there is a tacit assumption that people in their fifties and sixties are less productive and capable of learning than younger employees. With longer lives and longer careers there is an urgent need to view how others age differently. A failure to do so will prevent the opportun-ities and benefits that longevity brings from being realised.

Be aware that age-based stereotypes aren't just a prejudice against others, they are also a prejudice against your own future self. This will inevitably limit your long-term opportunities and the extent of your 'possible selves'. You might imagine talking to your eighty-year-old self or practise being 'age agnostic' in your choice of friends and acquaintances. Spending time with people of other ages helps you build a stronger narrative that links you with your future self.

REIMAGINING TIME

As healthy life expectancy increases, you have more time ahead of you. Whether you seize the advantages of this will depend on how you conceive of, and reimagine, time.

Future time

Your perspective on time could be that of Figure 3.3. You can imagine standing on the peak of a hill with the future ahead and the past behind you. In this *hilltop perspective*, the immediate present is larger and more prominent than any other moment in time, either past or future. The further down the hill you look, the smaller and more remote a unit of time seems. Your focus is on where you are now and the next few steps you will take.

FIGURE 3.3 A hilltop perspective on time

You are experiencing what behavioural economists call 'present bias',[10] and in making decisions about how to allocate time across your life you are focused on pay-offs and events closest to the present time.

An alternative time horizon is a *bird's-eye perspective*. Now you are looking down from above, and the terrain below appears flat. Every part of the terrain (both in the past and the present) looks equally important (Figure 3.4). Think of it as like looking down on a calendar – with each square representing moments, days, and years laid out alongside each other.

In a longer life this perspective has the advantage of putting more emphasis on your future self and thereby creating incentives to invest in future options, such as taking that gap year or spending time with children or learning a new skill. The longer your life the more future you have and so it makes sense to give it a greater weight as you think about the choices you face. In other words, be prepared to be more patient and to *discount* the future less.[11]

This perspective has profound implications on how you make decisions about allocating your time – across a week, a year, or even across your life as a whole.[12] It strengthens the links between activities at different moments in time and puts you in a better position to exploit the recursivity of age. The actions you take now help improve your chance of future success.

Figure 3.4 A bird's-eye perspective on time

The magic of compound interest

Longer horizons also enable you to take advantage of compounding. This may seem a famously dull subject but, given Albert Einstein referred to it as the eighth wonder of the world, it is worth spending some time understanding its implications.

Let's first think of compounding from a financial perspective. Imagine that at the age of twenty you invest $100 and have a 4 per cent return. By the time you are fifty that initial investment is $324, and by the time you are seventy it will have reached $711. Now, imagine that instead of investing at twenty, you leave it later – let's say at forty. By leaving it later to start, you will need to invest $219, not $100, to reach the same amount by the age of fifty. And if you leave it later still – at fifty, you would need to invest $324 to reach the same amount by seventy. The longer you leave your money invested, the more work is done by compound interest rather than you.

The magic of compounding is not just restricted to money. There are other forms of investments that could grow over time – investments in your skills, health and relationships. Take the case of investing in reskilling. Imagine you are fifty-five and only expect to work until you are sixty-five, then the return on investing in reskilling may not seem worthwhile. But now imagine you are aged fifty-five and expect to work until you are seventy-five. Suddenly it makes sense because of the accumulation impact – you have a longer time for the investment to pay back. The same is true in investing in health and fitness. If you are sixty and anticipate living to a hundred, then investing in your health and fitness now will attract greater 'compound interest' and therefore attract more 'dividends' than if you only lived to seventy.

In the present

Your decisions about the future allocation of time are made in the present. Your path forward will be constructed from the everyday choices you make now – and this never-ending sequence of decisions often has trade-offs to be made.

You know the feeling – you wake up in the morning not knowing how you are going to fit everything in. Frequently you don't. Instead, you focus on doing some activities today, push others back for tomorrow, and leave the rest for some time in the future. In other words, you are making trade-offs between various periods of time and by doing so implicitly deciding what matters most.

It's hard to make sensible decisions about the future when you feel pressured. These 'pinch points' can be particularly tough in the second stage of a traditional three-stage life. A three-stage life of education, work and retirement creates a specific approach to time trade-offs. During the first stage you have little money, but you are building up the skills to support your working career. In the second stage you have little leisure, but you work hard to finance retirement. In the third stage you run down your financial assets and enjoy leisure. This puts significant time pressures on the second stage and there is clear evidence that this can become a period of low psychological well-being.[13] During the second stage too many activities are competing against each other – working hard to establish a career, putting money aside for retirement, raising a family, looking after elderly parents, trying to maintain relationships, wondering about the purpose of life.

In a longer life you have the opportunity to reduce these pinch points by *redistributing* activities. When you redistribute core activities (education, work, retirement) across the whole of life then ultimately you reduce some of the time pressure, stress, and trade-offs that occur during each life stage. That means for example that time spent on education becomes a series of activities around lifetime learning; or that the 'downtime' of retirement is redistributed across life – in, for example, more time spent with your children as they grow up, or more time travelling and taking a gap year. There is much sense in this redistribution for, as studies show, when people overload activities into the hours of a single day, they become stressed and unhappy, but when these activities are redistributed over weeks or months, they feel a great deal happier.[14]

On the face of it, this redistribution appears relatively straightforward. The reality is that it's difficult to achieve. As we show later, some of the barriers to redistributing time are corporate practices that punish non-linear work narratives. But it is more than this: it is also about our own perspective on time.

Taking the long view can be difficult for all of us. But there are circumstances when the compulsion to focus only on the present becomes overwhelming. If the rent is due and it's another week until payday, it simply isn't practical or sensible advice to take the long view. That is how Estelle feels as she tries to financially support her children. She is aware of the value a college course could bring over time and feels the disadvantages of leaving school at sixteen with minimal qualifications. She'd like to qualify as a beautician with the idea of one day running her own beauty salon. But that is looking into the future, and right now the present is jostling for attention as she tries to earn money to pay her bills, look after her children, and be on standby in case she gets extra hours of work at the care home. For Estelle time is a very scarce resource, and that scarcity is likely to affect how she makes decisions.

As Harvard economist Sendhil Mullainathan and Princeton psychologist Eldar Shafir have shown,[15] when a resource is scarce, it dominates thinking and becomes the problem that has to be fixed. The result of this 'tunnelling' is that people become vulnerable to making bad decisions that can be costly in the long run. Estelle's worries about money and the cognitive 'tunnelling' effect that goes with it, is inevitably reducing her mental bandwidth. That means she is more likely to only focus on the immediate problems she faces and is prey to making bad decisions that have long-term implications. For instance, she has lately become reliant on payday loans, even though the interest rates and fees are extremely high.

The best counterbalance to tunnelling is 'slack' – the creation of a pool of resources that limit the distorting effects of scarcity on decision making. This slack can take a number of forms: it could be a pool of savings that can be dipped into; or building time out on a regular basis; or acquiring new skills that may be useful in the future or a baseline level of fitness. These are all ways to build precautionary balances that provide a buffer in the event of bad future circumstances. This in turn will help stave off scarcity and enable you to make better future decisions.

It also makes sense to think in terms of 'nudges'. To set things up so that the right decision doesn't require time and focus. This might be saying, for example, that every time you pay the rent you put an extra $5 aside into a pot, or that every week you leave Tuesday afternoon clear of meetings. In a longer life establishing these sorts of habits early on provides a foundation for preparing for the future.

The tunnel of work

One of the hardest, but potentially most invigorating, aspects of moving away from a three-stage life is managing the trade-offs between work and leisure. In the second stage of a three-stage life it is work that dominates. But as people live longer and have more years, then to make full use of extra years there will be times when you could and should trade off work for leisure. But it isn't just corporate practices that may prevent this, it is also your own propensity of tunnelling around the importance of work.

At a Cambridge University conference on 'the Future of Work', held in 2016, we were struck by a comment that Brendan Burchell of the Judge Business School made about this: 'If you buy a pack of paracetamol from a pharmacy, it will tell you on the packet how many pills you need to take. With regards to paid work, however, no study has revealed how much you need to do to get the full benefits. It may be far less than we are used to doing now: perhaps as low as 8 to 15 hours a week.'[16]

Historically the richest members of society, the 'leisure class', worked considerably fewer hours than those on lower pay.[17] Now it's those with the highest pay who work the longest hours – they are trading leisure for money. Why the change? It could be that when people are paid significantly for every hour they work, then taking time off is expensive; or these highly paid jobs are more competitive and therefore more prone to 'presentism' – people simply need to be seen to be productive; or perhaps people find this higher paid work more enjoyable and meaningful, and so shift their time from less enjoyable tasks to more enjoyable work. Declining higher rates of tax have also made work more financially remunerative for the well paid.

But these choices have profound implications – particularly the danger of overwork and the failure to redistribute leisure time from the end of life into midlife. This is worth considering, particularly in view of the evidence of the dark side of overwork as well as the positive impact of periods of recovery.

As we live longer, our careers will be longer and that creates opportunities to make trade-offs between time at work and time with family. To illustrate the dilemmas this creates, here is a trade-off question that the UCLA's Hal Hershfield and co-authors posed to 4,000 people: 'Imagine you are a university professor invited to teach a weekend seminar out of state. But you have a baby girl at home, born 12 weeks earlier. The pay you receive from the seminar would offset the costs of childcare, but it means you would not spend the weekend with your new baby girl – what choice would you make?'[18]

This is a direct work/time and family/time trade-off. How would you go about thinking through this choice? Clearly the value of the money is easy to quantify. But you probably found it harder to put a value on the time that would be lost with the family. In putting a value on it – a longer life creates an interesting perspective on this trade-off. It inevitably shifts it towards spending time with the baby. As Hershfield notes, 'there are only 222 weekends left before the baby would start kinder-garten, when quality family hours would give way to car pools to friends' houses'.[19] The nature of this trade-off changes as we live and work longer. For whilst the number of possible weekends with the baby doesn't increase, the number of weekends of conferences and meetings certainly does. So, on balance, spending time with the baby is more valuable, you have plenty of time later in life to attend work meetings. Exploiting these changes in the trade-off between work and family is at the heart of redistributing time in a multistage life.

REIMAGINING A JOB

In the rhythm of our narratives, one of the major defining notes are our current and future jobs. In navigating your life story, work can meet a foundational need: to provide resources to secure a good standard of living. But for most of us, work plays another role: it shapes our identity and creates much of the context of daily life. This sense of identity is currently being reshaped by technological ingenuity, which is fundamentally disrupting jobs and work.

Tom has mixed feelings about his job. On the positive side it gives him a steady and reasonable income, he enjoys being on the road and likes the familiarity and routine the job provides. But on his long-haul trips he misses his family and worries about his aging parents. Like many of his fellow truck drivers, Tom is overweight, the result of too many diner stops, and his doctor is warning him about the risks of diabetes. As Tom gets older, he's finding it hard to sleep when he is travelling, and his sedentary life is starting to take its toll on his body. Tom had planned a safe retirement but has heard his union recently cut retirement benefits by 30 per cent in order to improve the scheme's sustainability.

Across the world in Sydney, Ying has some of these worries. She's furious that the accountancy firm she has worked with for much of her life has asked her to leave. She will miss the job and the camaraderie, and she also needs another source of income. One of the reasons Ying is being let go by her firm is the investment they have made in accounting software. This software is capable of processing thousands of tax returns in milliseconds – something it would have taken well-paid Ying weeks to accomplish.

We are not the first humans to be anxious about how technology will change our jobs. Yet as every economics textbook will tell you, historically new technologies have always eventually led to higher standards of living and haven't created aggregate unemployment. However, to simply assume this will be the case now is dangerous. The impact of technology on jobs is complicated and we cannot simply look to history to understand the next couple of decades.

Engel's pause

Tom and Ying are part of a massive transition in the nature and form of work. To give a sense of the scale, consider the estimate that by 2030 between 75 and 375 million people may need to switch their occupation and learn new skills – that's 14 per cent of all workers.[20]

The impact of transitions of this scale can be understood through the example of the Industrial Revolution in the UK. As economist and Nobel Laureate Paul Krugman remarked about this transition: 'Mechanisation eventually – that is after a couple of generations – led to a broad rise in British living standards. But it's far from clear whether typical workers reaped any benefits during the early stages of the Industrial Revolution; many workers were clearly hurt.'[21] Note his time frame – 'a couple of generations'. It is what economic historian Bob Allen calls 'Engel's pause' – the observation that during the first half of the Industrial Revolution, despite rising productivity, pay stagnated and inequality increased. It wasn't just those who lost their jobs who lost out during the Industrial Revolution.[22]

There are already signs that something similar may be happening during the current transition. Take for example the share of the economy that gets paid out to workers (the 'labour share'). This has fallen in the US steadily from around 65 per cent in the early 1990s to around 60 per cent in 2018. That may not sound significant, but it's a big shift historically. The income that used to get paid to workers is now paid to the owners of the firms using or producing the machines, and the software that replaced workers, or to those workers with the skills that are enhanced and augmented by technology. Looking forward, it is likely that even if Tom keeps his job as a truck driver he could be paid less. It will be the manufacturer of autonomous trucks who gets paid more, and the software engineers they employ.

In other words, it isn't just the 14 per cent of workers who are expected to lose their job that will potentially be impacted as AI and robotics transform the workplace. The remaining 86 per cent will also be affected, and they have the anxiety that they *may* lose their job, whilst some will find their job redesigned and their wages fall. The issues around your work narrative therefore go far deeper than whether you will have a job. To understand this complexity, let's take a closer look at what is likely to happen to Tom.

Tom's dilemma

Tom is one of 4 million people in the US who work in driving occupations. As a consequence of the mass digitalisation of data, the exponential increase in computational power and improvements in algorithms, autonomous vehicles are a reality that makes Tom fear for his job. But if we examine Tom's situation more closely, we can see that technology, jobs, labour markets and demography interact in complex ways. That makes it difficult to draw a simple connection between automation and job losses.

Most labour markets (such as that for truck drivers) experience a great deal of turnover every year and this doesn't necessarily lead to higher unemployment. Whilst the media places much focus on the *level* of unemployment, considerably less attention is paid to the number of *new jobs* being created each year and the number of *jobs being destroyed* (either through 'quits' or redundancies). A glance at the total US labour force data for 2018 gives us an idea of how substantial this labour market turnover is. In that year, 149 million people were employed and a total of 68.9 million new jobs created, whilst 66.1 million jobs came to an end.[23] In other words – job losses don't automatically lead to higher unemployment.

This is apparent in Tom's industry. In the transportation sector, the total annual job separations (people leaving their job either voluntarily or through redundancy) is approximately 40 per cent of the number of people employed. As a result, a major challenge for trucking firms is they cannot recruit and retain enough drivers. Currently there is a shortfall of 50,000 drivers[24] and that's expected to increase to 175,000 by 2024. The reasons behind this shortfall are many, but in part it's a consequence of the demographics of an aging society. Tom, aged forty, is relatively young in an industry where less than 20 per cent of drivers are under the age of thirty-five. As the large cohort of those in their fifties and sixties approach retirement, the trucking sector will require close to one million new drivers just to keep pace with demand.

Viewed in this light, headline figures of job losses from automation are overstated. This holds even more acutely for countries such as China and Japan, where the working age population is forecast to fall by 300 million and 32 million respectively over the next three decades. In these cases, where the workforce is declining, robots can't come fast enough.

But to really understand the impact of machines on your current or future job, you also need to distinguish between a *job* and the *tasks* that make up that job. Machines perform tasks and a job is made up of many tasks. Whether your job is at risk therefore depends on what type of tasks you perform and how many of them are vulnerable to automation. Initially researchers investigating job losses from automation assumed that a job consisted of a small set of defined tasks. This led to very high estimates of the number of jobs which would be impacted by machines. However, in reality most jobs are made up of multiple types of activities or tasks.[25] Think about your own job – ours, for example, includes writing books and academic papers, reviewing peer articles, speaking at conferences and seminars, preparing and presenting lectures and grading student scripts, as well as attending any number of meetings.

This distinction between jobs and tasks is important because, whilst machines will undoubtedly replace *many* of the tasks involved in Tom's job, it's unlikely they will replace *all* of them. In our case, for example, we look forward to AI that can effectively grade student scripts or prepare (and even deliver) our lectures. As these separate tasks are automated the focus of the tasks that make up our job will change. For instance, as grading takes up less time the senior team at London Business School could respond by requiring greater research output from its professors (and probably more meetings).

In Tom's case, autonomous vehicles currently struggle to drive in cities, especially during inclement weather conditions, or over unpredictable terrain. That suggests that automation may lead to Tom's job no longer including the task of driving on a highway, but it could include the task of navigating around cities. And at both ends of the journey there are manual tasks that the truck itself is incapable of doing – again providing opportunities for Tom. And even if automation could perform all of Tom's current tasks, full automation will be delayed by a host of legal and regulatory issues along with issues around the cultural acceptance of AI and politically motivated policy aimed at protecting jobs. Whilst trials of autonomous trucks have already commenced between Texas and California, they still require a human driver and can only operate on highways.

What makes it difficult to accurately predict when and how autonomous vehicles will be introduced is that it depends in part on whether the vehicles will be partially or fully autonomous. It would seem that partial automatisation is more likely in the short to medium term, meaning that Tom should expect to eventually work as a 'co-pilot' or 'virtual driver' based at a central location. Tom's generation of truck drivers will most likely work in collaboration with AI, rather than being completely replaced.

We therefore expect that Tom will have a job in the near future. But what it means to be a truck driver will change as he effectively shifts roles and undergoes a transition, impacting on his life narrative and the choices he faces. This change in the nature of his job is also likely to have an effect on his pay. He may not earn what he used to if the role and the tasks he performs are less valuable. The more his job resembles his current job, but with greater assistance from technology, the less Tom is likely to earn. Alternatively, the more his job gets upgraded skills-wise – so that he becomes the controller of a highly sophisticated piece of electrical machinery – the more he is likely to earn.

So what can Tom do now? One option is that he continues on his current path as a truck driver. In the schema shown earlier in Figure 3.1, his future narrative simply flows forward in a straight line from his current position. Or Tom could take another path – decide to reskill and take advantage of an expanding autonomous truck industry that will need specially trained mechanics to maintain them. Tom has other possible paths: he could apply for a job in the warehouse where many of his friends work, accumulating new skills and experiences. Ultimately the path that Tom takes now will lead him to different future platforms and will change his possible future paths and possible selves.

How should Tom make this choice? At the moment he would prefer to remain a trucker than work in the warehouse, he wants to stay on the path he is already on. He can imagine being an engine mechanic, but he is worried about whether he could learn the trade and afford the fees for the qualification. That would be a more innovative path but also has risks associated with it. If Tom looks forward and understands something about the scale and scope of automation, then he will inevitably be concerned that if he remains a trucker he will be closing down future paths. If he's fired in five years' time when automation is really significant, he may be scrambling to find another option and won't have invested in the qualification or experience for the job in an engine shop.

These abrupt endings are problematic because they take away the opportunity to plan and prepare, narrowing future options. If Tom is to make the switch it would make sense to make it earlier rather than later, given that people who make the career switch earliest tend to benefit the most. He has to consider not just immediate actions, but also the impact several stages ahead. That means he needs to gain insight now about where his decisions today might lead.

The future of jobs

Tom's job as a truck driver reveals many of the nuances of how technology will impact the labour market. But what can you expect?

Given the complexities involved, it is perhaps not surprising there is no consensus on the *net* impact of technology on jobs. A Pew Research Center study found a 52:48 split between experts who think machines will replace more jobs than they will create and those who believe the opposite.[26] In general, technologists have the more pessimistic forecasts on jobs since they focus on how rapidly AI is developing and the potential this implies for job losses. Economists are more optimistic: they note that technology has never created mass unemployment before and believe technologists exaggerate how rapidly automation will be implementable on a cost-effective basis. Further, the economists argue, while it is relatively easy to see the jobs that will be *destroyed*, it's much harder to anticipate the *new jobs* that will be created by new technologies, new markets and new products.

In understanding this more deeply we find it useful to refer to the framework created by MIT's Daron Acemoglu and Boston University's Pascual Restrepo.[27] Their view is that individual jobs and the wider labour market are impacted in part by a *displacement* effect: as automation replaces tasks, firms need fewer workers. To understand this for your own job you need to consider the potential size of this displacement effect. The more your job is made up of routine tasks, the greater its risk from automation. So in our jobs for example, there are routine tasks (e.g. marking scripts and making slides for presentations), as well as complex tasks (e.g. developing research hypotheses, mentoring doctorate students). Whilst each job has its own unique mix of routine and complex tasks, studies estimate that in general across the whole labour market, around half of tasks embedded within jobs are routine and therefore relatively easy to automate.[28] However, only around 5 per cent of jobs are made up of tasks in which 90–100 per cent of the tasks can be automated. This helps explain why past automation has displaced relatively few jobs. Since the 1950s, only one of 270 occupations listed in the US census has been completely eliminated as a consequence of automation – elevator operator.[29]

While most jobs are not capable of full automation, many (around 60 per cent) have about a third of their constituent tasks that are easy to automate. In jobs in accommodation and food services, the potential for the automation of tasks is high (estimates of around 75 per cent). In manufacturing, transportation, warehousing and agriculture around 60 per cent of tasks could be automated; and in retail trade and mining it is about half of the tasks. There are other jobs where the percentage of tasks that could be automated is much lower. These jobs are in sectors such as education (around 25 per cent) where teaching, mentoring and coaching are less likely to be automated. They are also jobs in management (again coaching, mentoring and directing tasks), professionals (such as lawyers and consultants), and health care (nurses, general practitioners, surgeons).

When you think about your own job, or the job you would like to do in the future, it is impossible to create an accurate timetable of automation – there are just too many unknowns. But you can take an educated guess by being alert to the changes and noticing the speed at which these processes unfold. In particular, consider the four barriers to automation that could stop your job being completely automated. The first is the extent to which your job is made up of tasks that are *non-routine* – which will determine how difficult it is to automate. Next is whether you will have opportunities to shift into higher-value-added tasks, which are tasks that are on the higher ground of Moravec's landscape of human competence – such as empathy, relating, judgement or creativity. You will also need to consider whether you are well placed to get these new opportunities in terms of your existing skills. Third is the environment of the job – for example will regulation, such as concerns over safety or the need for human overrides, act as a barrier to automation? And finally, will it be cost-effective to automate your job? For instance, the AlphaGo technology we described earlier is impressive but also requires enormous, expensive computing power. What matters is not whether a machine can do your job, but whether it can do it more cheaply.

The speed at which the tasks within your job will be automated depends on how substantial these barriers are for you. If these barriers are not in place, then you can expect automation to impact your role rapidly in the next two to three years. But remember that even if the barriers are high, you are likely to experience a substantial change in how you perform your job in the next ten years.

The second effect in the Acemoglu and Restrepo framework is the impact of rising *productivity*. Whilst automation replaces some tasks, it also helps workers become more productive and more profitable, and this encourages firms to hire more of them. In other words, technology augments humans rather than replaces them. So whilst, for example in the US, 400,000 bookkeeping jobs were lost in the wake of the introduction of VisiCalc, 600,000 accounting jobs were created. Because it was cheaper and quicker to perform calculations, firms could therefore create more data and higher-quality financial insights, and this raised the productivity of those jobs based on the analysis of data. As a consequence, more accountants were hired. Similarly, the number of bank cashiers actually increased in response to the introduction of ATMs. These machines freed bank cashiers and assistants from performing low-value tasks such as dispensing cash to customers and gave them more time for higher-value activities such as assisting customers with more complex problems and cross-selling a range of banking products and services. This switch to higher-value tasks in turn resulted in branches becoming more productive and so led to an increase in the number of bank cashiers.[30]

What is important here is that whilst across the whole labour market this productivity effect has a positive impact on employment, it inevitably involves a significant shift in the nature of the job and the skills required. Not every bank cashier was able to become a relationship manager, and not every book clerk became an accountant.

As automation augments worker productivity, some will receive higher wages. Tom's supervisor now has a graduate degree in data analytics and is getting paid a salary far greater than his predecessor as his job has moved from simple scheduling to optimisation. Ying's manager's responsibilities grew as the department was consolidated and her salary increased as a consequence. Those people who decide to upskill in order to shift their role into more profitable tasks and away from those that become automated are also likely to be the ones who will benefit from these higher wages.

The third and final effect in the Acemoglu and Restrepo model is the *creation of new types of jobs*. Some of these new jobs will be highly complex. Tom's adult son has a real interest in technology and his dream is to work on the cutting edge of AI. There is a whole range of new jobs in AI: he could apply to be a 'trainer' (a data scientist who builds the algorithms on which AI programs are trained), an 'explainer' (a communications job which involves communicating and explaining the algorithms that underlie the AI decision-making, and then explaining the outcomes) or a 'sustainer' (repairing, maintaining and developing AI systems).[31] And if you weren't already convinced of the extent of this new wave of jobs, a 2017 McKinsey Global Institute study predicted that by 2030, between 20–50 million digital jobs globally could be created.[32]

But it would also be a mistake to assume that all the new jobs created will be in the digital and technology sector. As more time is dedicated to helping people age better there will be rising demand for fitness coaches and yoga teachers. And as people put lifelong learning at the centre of their lives, there will be more jobs available as career counsellors and life coaches. We will also be prepared to pay more to experience human creativity and entertainment. McKinsey predicts an increased demand for creative work – for artists, designers, entertainers and media workers. This is a global phenomenon: by 2030, the demand for these skills is predicted to rise by 85 per cent in China and 58 per cent in India. These new jobs are in addition to those that will come from the needs of a rising proportion of older people, and the job creation resulting from significant investments in renewable energy and adaption to climate change.

A FLUID CAREER

Jobs and work make up the daily activities of a working life – viewed across time they become the basis of a career. As the framing of this time shifts from a three-stage to a multistage life, so careers become more fluid.

More years

Part of this career fluidity results from the increased length of working life. In *The 100-Year Life* we calculated that if you have a life expectancy of a hundred years and save 10 per cent of your salary, then you will be working into your late seventies or early eighties in order to finance a pension worth half of your final salary.[33] MIT economist Jim Poterba calculates that every ten years of extra life expectancy requires seven more years of working in order to finance retirement (based on current interest rates and pension levels). So, based on the increase in UK life expectancy since 1981, current fifty-year-olds should plan on working at least to between sixty-eight and seventy-two years of age.

You can expect government policy to adapt to longer lives by steadily increasing the state pension age. Take the UK, for example, where in the 1920s the pension age for men was sixty-five and sixty for women; by 1995 the government announced the closing of the gender gap, with women's pensions slowly rising to sixty-five; and in 2019 it announced that between 2044 and 2046 the pension age would be raised to sixty-eight for both men and women. The UK government has gone so far as to provide guidance on how future retirement age will change as longevity increases: it announced that the state retirement age will not change by more than one year in a decade, and people can expect to be eligible for a pension for one-third of their adult life.

69

In China, the rapid increase in life expectancy will inevitably mean substantial changes to the pensionable age, which is currently sixty for men, fifty-five for women white-collar workers and fifty for women blue-collar workers. There are proposals to increase the age that women retire by one year every three years, and by one year every six years for men. On current projections, by 2045 the retirement age for both men and women would be sixty-five. Such increases are not without their political consequences. In 2018, on the first day of their hosting the FIFA World Cup, the Russian government announced an increase in state pension age from sixty to sixty-five for men and fifty-five to sixty-three for women. The subsequent political protest led to a record slump in President Putin's approval ratings, with 90 per cent of citizens against the reform.

Such increases in the state pension age only tell part of the story. Many people are already choosing to work longer. In Japan, the state pension can be drawn at any age between sixty and seventy, and the longer a citizen leaves it, the greater the pension they receive. However, more than 30 per cent of Japanese aged between 70–74 are still working. In the US it's 20 per cent and in the UK just over 10 per cent and in both countries the proportion is rising. Working into your seventies, and possibly in some capacity into your eighties, looks set to eventually become the norm as careers elongate and become more fluid.

This may sound a daunting prospect, but it's not all bad news. In fact, there is evidence that working extends healthy living. Indeed, for jobs which don't involve physical labour, it seems that the later you retire the longer you live. A study of nearly three thousand people who had retired between 1992 and 2010 compared the risk of dying for those who retired at aged 65, at 67, at 70, and at 72. For each two years of work, people survived longer than the cohort that retired earlier. Specifically, working to sixty-seven reduces the risk of dying by over 20 per cent; working to seventy compared to sixty-five reduces the risk of dying at seventy by 44 per cent; and working to seventy-two sees a 56 per cent fall in the probability of dying at that age.[34] These positive effects of working longer may explain the recent 'unretiring' trend. In the UK 1 in 4 people who retire at sixty-five 'unretire' within five years[35] – pioneers in a multistage life.

Increased leisure time

Not all the additional years of life will be spent working, and so that means more leisure time. In a three-stage life leisure time was primarily allocated at the end of life, in retirement. In a multistage life there is an opportunity to redistribute these extra years throughout life, perhaps taking a gap year, as part of a mid-career transition, or as a short period around sixty-five before 'unretiring'.

The redistribution of this additional leisure time need not be restricted to large blocks of time, such as months and years. It can also be redistributed to shorter periods of time, such as fewer working hours in a day, or a three-day weekend. Behind this optimism is a simple economic logic: as technology boosts human productivity it makes each hour worked more productive and helps raise income. And as humans become richer, they want more of all things – including leisure.[36] Therefore thanks to the miracle of productivity growth, people consume more *and* work less and see their standard of living rise. This trend has played out over modern history. For instance, in 1870 the average German worked sixty-eight hours a week and the average American sixty-two. By 2000 this had fallen to forty-one and forty-three respectively.[37] Higher levels of productivity over time led to shorter working weeks.

This implies that if AI and robotics have the same impact as past technologies, it is likely that we will eventually see a four-day working week/three-day weekend. There is already some evidence from companies who have adopted the four-day working week that it is associated with improvements in productivity and employee well-being.[38] For now, only those firms with most flexible working practices are likely to succeed with a four-day working week, but as more firms participate it could well become a new norm in the decades ahead.

In the most utopian visions of technological progress, machines become so productive that humans have no need for paid work and ample opportunities for extended leisure. Erik Brynjolfsson of MIT calls this a 'Digital Athens', referring to the intellectual flowering of Athens when slaves freed the great thinkers – Socrates, Aristotle and Plato – to devote their time to pondering deep philosophical issues. In a world of smart machines, it is digital slaves who could free humans from the drudgery of work, enabling them to pursue their own interests and passions – taking up more meaningful and engaging self-driven activities such as craft-based work or volunteering. Of course, this is an extreme case where humans will need to fashion a dramatically new sense of narrative. But even if society does not reach this utopian state, we will still need to carve out room for more leisure time.

More alternative work

The current dominant concept of work is a full-time job in a stable and secure arrangement. People provide their labour services in a guaranteed and relatively permanent way in exchange for money and other benefits. And whilst being a full-time employee is likely to remain a common pattern of work, in a more fluid career it would be wise to assume that many people at some stage will experience contingent or alternative forms of work. Whether it's a way of earning additional money, managing periods of transition or overcoming corporate ageism and working later in life, you should anticipate taking on this type of work at some point in your life.

This could range from freelancing (as Radhika does), to temporary work agencies (as Estelle sometimes uses), to on demand part-time work, and more recently gig work. What distinguishes these from more traditional patterns of work is that they are based on short-term relationships between the firm and the worker, where the worker is paid only for the tasks they perform, and an expectation that the job will come to an end sometime soon. Since the 1990s, more than half of the jobs created across the OECD countries have been contingent jobs. However, whilst many new jobs are contingent, it is important to realise

72

that across the total US employment market in 2017 they still only represent around 10 per cent of total employment.[39]

Radhika is a contingent worker. She doesn't work full-time for any one employer, but rather works for a whole range of employers in project-based activities. This type of work has been made possible by ever-more sophisticated working platforms that connect, with as little friction as possible, those who want tasks to be completed with those who have the skills to complete them. Online platforms such as Freelancer and Upwork provide this service, and we can imagine many more platforms like this developing. While these online platforms that Radhika uses, as well as others like TaskRabbit and Uber, are growing rapidly, they still only account for less than 1 per cent of US workers. There is a lot more future growth possible.

Technological innovations have made these platforms feasible and have also facilitated the unbundling of jobs into separate, standardised tasks. These tasks can then be allocated to various workers, rather than to one worker. Technology also enables a worker's performance to be monitored and profiled against others. Freelancers like Radhika perform very specific tasks – say, writing an article or producing a web page. She is not an 'employee' and has to create her own sense of a 'job' by performing these tasks for a multiplicity of clients. That means that her working patterns are very different from Tom, who has a broad range of responsibilities that he is aware of and replicates on a daily basis. Radhika operates in an open market bidding for well-defined tasks or projects. That means she has more autonomy and flexibility than Tom in what she decides to take on and when she performs her work. But there are also downsides – every day she worries about the next contract and wonders about the companionship that a more traditional job might bring.

How you will feel about contingent work will depend in part on your motivation and why you are taking it up.[40] Around 30 per cent are 'free agents' like Radhika, attracted by the freedom and flexibility that the work provides. About 40 per cent are 'casual earners', looking to boost their household earnings beyond their main source of income. Both of these groups tend to be satisfied with the nature of their work and role, leaving about 30 per cent who are 'reluctant' and who would prefer a full-time position.

Ying falls into this final 'reluctant' category. She would prefer full-time work and worries that if she becomes a freelancer her wages will fall and the work will have less prestige. Estelle works at the care home to boost her income – she's a 'casual earner', financially strapped and thinking about signing up as an Uber driver. She is tempted by the Uber adverts which describe extra money and more freedom but is worried about financing a car and how she would juggle her current jobs and childcare. She can't yet see how it could work for her.

There is a view that platform 'gig' work, like Uber or Deliveroo, is 'bad work'. It's often relatively low-skilled and low-paid, so people have to work long hours, and by doing so lose much of the freedom and autonomy that is a major attraction of contingent work. The same holds for freelance work. A glance at the websites of either Freelance.com or Upwork show this is work that is generally paid by the hour at modest rates. It is also episodic, with projects lasting from anything from a few hours to a few days, and rarely longer than that. This means that finding work becomes a weekly or even daily activity, making it hard to plan for the future. Moreover, because most contingent workers are not classified as employees, they currently have little or no holiday entitlements, pension arrangements or health care provision. Brandeis University's David Weil describes the result as 'the fissured workplace', where companies use contingent workers to streamline and boost their profitability and transfer their obligations over pay, safety and benefits outside of the firm. As a consequence, 'sustaining the employer–worker relationship ranks far below the value of building a devoted customer base and delivering value to investors'[41].

As this contingent work becomes more prevalent, companies will become more mindful of how best to use it. Already some are discovering that if they frequently use the same contractors, it makes sense to provide some form of training around corporate values and standards. Rather than viewing them as a pool of 'contingent workers' they are seen as their 'bench strength', available to be incorporated into specific projects or during peak times. So over the course of your working life, expect your relationship with your employer to have considerable variation – from contracted employee, project-based worker, or 'on the bench' freelancer.

A broader sense of work

The schema of your future paths and possible selves is sure to take on a more fluid structure as you cycle in and out of connectedness with your employers. There will be times when you will take a distinct role in a conventional job. There will be times when you perform very specific tasks on a contingent basis in work that is more flexible and autonomous, but where there are greater risks of financial insecurity and a weaker sense of identity. At times you will work in an office or a factory, and at other times you will work from home.

The fundamental implication of this more fluid career structure is that you are taking more responsibility, more personal agency. This is a career that is less a joint enterprise between you and an employer who is prepared to take responsibility for upgrading your skills, planning your next stage, making financial preparations for your future and investigating possible options. There are activities that will be increasingly your responsibility. This means that the time you spend 'working' will expand beyond simply paid hours to encompass the time you invest in building your current or future resources – developing additional skills to support your next stage of work; spending time investigating alternative career paths; taking time in community-based activities in a Digital Athens. This is why the capacity and courage to redistributing time is so crucial. In a three-stage life there is a simple dichotomy between paid work and unpaid leisure. In a flexible, multistage life there is an enhanced sense of individual responsibility and personal agency and a broader sense of 'work'.

WHAT MAKES FOR A GOOD LIFE?

Our focus so far has been on how technology and longevity will change the structure of your narrative – making it longer and with more stages and embracing various permutations of work, leisure, life and finances. Yet any narrative requires not just a structure, but also a unifying theme and purpose. The motivation behind your narrative has to be, what is it that makes for a good life?

Clearly money matters – and there is no doubt that in a hundred-year life there is an urgency to earn enough of it to finance a good retirement, a healthy lifestyle and support breaks for lifelong learning and recuperation.

Consider the words of the Dalai Lama, who when asked what surprised him about humanity answered 'Man – he sacrifices his health in order to make money. Then he sacrifices money to recuperate his health. And then he is so anxious about the future that he does not enjoy the present; the result being that he does not live in the present or the future; he lives as if he is never going to die and then dies having never really lived.' For the Dalai Lama money and happiness are unrelated.[42]

Turning from the Dalai Lama to the more prosaic world of empirical research, it seems in general the more money a person has, or the higher a country's income, then in general the happier they and the population are. However, it's not quite that simple. There are outliers – the population of Costa Rica for example are happier than those in Hong Kong, despite having lower income. And it seems that money suffers from diminishing returns. An extra £1,000 when you earn £60,000 doesn't have the same uplifting effect on happiness as an extra £1,000 has if your income is £20,000. This doesn't mean that money stops making you happier, it just becomes a less powerful force.

There is also much debate about the nature of happiness. The Greek philosopher Epicurus believed happiness was about pleasure and the avoidance of bad experiences; whilst Aristotle, in his concept of 'eudaimonia' (or human flourishing) described the essence of happiness as purpose and well-being. Again, turning to empirical research, two Nobel Prize winners – the economist

Angus Deaton and the psychologist Daniel Kahneman – explored happiness and money in a large survey of Americans.[43] They discovered that when it came to day-to-day happiness, above an income of $75,000, people with more money were no more satisfied.[44] However, with regard to purpose, in general richer people expressed greater satisfaction with their life. This is how Deaton and Kahneman summarise their results: 'high income brings life satisfaction but not happiness, and low income is associated both with low life satisfaction and low emotional well-being'. This suggests that while money may not be the path to happiness it is an important pillar in supporting a good life.

However, broader studies that explore happiness and satisfaction across a whole life find another crucial variable. The nature of that variable was highlighted in the Grant Study based at Harvard Medical School, which engaged with the same cohort of 268 people over seventy-five years – from their graduation from Harvard between 1939–44 (including amongst them John F. Kennedy). This cohort was later supplemented with an additional group of 456 disadvantaged Boston inner city youths.

The focus of the Grant Study was the causality of life satisfaction, and indeed those people with more money tended to be happier. However, it turned out that, while important, money was not the most important factor for a satisfied and happy life. The greatest impact on life satisfaction came from the 'warmth of relationships'. In the words of George Valliant, the director of the study: 'Happiness is love. Full stop.' It seems that connecting with others is fundamental to a good life and having the means to cope with the challenges that life creates.

A similar message also emerged from Hal Hershfield's study of whether people would choose to stay at home with their baby daughter or get paid to attend a weekend conference. In that study, 65 per cent of people chose the money, yet it turned out that those who chose family time were on average happier and more satisfied with life. Why might this be the case? Hershfield's suggestion is that those who chose money over time are more likely to be fixated on not having *enough* money. Those who chose time over money focused more on how they would *spend* their time, planning to 'spend' it on wants rather than needs (e.g. cultivating a hobby versus completing chores at home). In particular they often planned to spend their time with other people rather than themselves.

As you reflect on these various insights about happiness, consider how in a multistage life you have the chance at different stages to build a variety of resources. This is important as it creates the opportunity to transfer these resources to later periods in life. One of these resources will certainly be money, but it won't always be the main resource. There may be certain points in life when the best way to boost your future pension will not be to save more money, but rather to invest that money and time in learning and education. Or to redistribute time from the future to the present to support friendships and building relationships.

Achieving financial security will be an important goal in a longer life, but the return on other activities (such as purpose, engagement, health, relationships) has to be factored in. Beware of jeopardising your future self by not spending sufficient time in these other activities, as much as you should be focusing on jeopardising your finances. In other words, it is important that it isn't just financial plans that drive your narrative, but rather that it is your narrative that drives the financial plans.

YOUR NARRATIVE

Sketch possible selves

We began with a generic sketch of 'possible selves' and then considered Tom's life course – the possible paths ahead of him and the options he faced. It may be worthwhile going through the same exercise for yourself – imagining what a path into the future could look like for you, and then testing it against a number of assumptions and questions.

Examine your underlying assumptions

Be aware that longevity, technology and social change all require you to develop a new narrative that is not simply based on past assumptions. This new narrative is longer and contains more segments that have numerous ways of being sequenced. Your career will extend much further, but it will also carry a greater risk of abrupt endings.

Will there be abrupt endings? In the earlier discussion of technological innovation, we showed how the pathways of Tom and Ying are likely to be impacted by automation and indeed could come to an abrupt ending. What is the likelihood that any of the paths you have sketched would come to an abrupt end? If that were to happen, are the platforms you would have developed by this time sufficiently broad to enable you to adapt to another path?

Is my thinking too constrained and narrow? Are there other options that you have not considered or wider options that are available to you? Could you be more experimental and courageous in your actions? Are your networks too narrow and constraining? The more you are able to consider experimental paths, the more you will be able to engage with the future through a process of discovery.

Am I making the wrong assumptions about age? Take a look at the pathways you are considering and the stages you have described. Have you inadvertently made the wrong assumptions about your own future age and process of aging? Are you basing your assumptions too much on chronological age? Have you closed down your options too early and run the risk of being 'old before your time'?

Am I factoring in institutional change? Inevitably your future narratives are anchored in your experiences of the present and the past. Much could change in the institutions that frame your future narrative – in terms of corporate practice, educational opportunities and government policy. Check that your possible paths into the future are taking into account the sort of institutional changes we will explore in Part III.

Consider time allocation

Time is one of the most precious resources you will have and using it wisely will be crucial.

Could I redistribute time? Thinking about each of your possible paths and the stages in these paths, would it be possible to rearrange the activities in these stages so that they give you more time? That could mean, for example, that rather than concentrating all these activities into a single stage, you could break them up into smaller pieces of time and redistribute them more evenly across the path of your whole life.

On what basis am I allocating time? As you consider each of the pathways consider what the fundamental driver of time allocation in each is. Are you planning to allocate time, for example, on acquiring money, broadening skills or taking time with family and friends? Is this the right allocation? You need to consider whether any of these paths runs the risk of jeopardising your future self.

Lastly, remember that your narrative is *recursive* in the sense that the actions you take today will determine the platform and choices available to you in the future. This is a strong argument against determinism: at any point in your life it is possible to take positive actions that impact your future.

4

EXPLORE: LEARNING AND TRANSITIONING

The first sighting of a driverless vehicle on the streets of Texas was a newsworthy event – it gave Tom a clear warning that he would need to think again about his truck-driving job. Yet much technological innovation goes unnoticed; each year, cumulative developments push forward the frontier of what is possible. That's the case for Ying. There was never a time when she *saw* the future as Tom did, when he first spotted that autonomous vehicle. Instead, over time, the tasks that defined her job became increasingly automated.

Now faced with the prospect of redundancy Ying is being forced to *explore* and learn something new. There are many paths she could take, each of which would result in a different 'possible self'. She needs to explore, to discover her preferences and the path that will take her towards her chosen future self. She knows the transition will not be easy and the sense of setting off in a new and uncertain direction is hard at a time when she is still dealing with the shock of her imminent redundancy.

Hiroki is also exploring. His father left college and went to work for a large company where he still works today – his was the classic three-stage life of education, then work, followed by retirement. Yet as Hiroki looks ahead at what could be a sixty-year career, he's not sure he wants to commit to the same career path. Like Ying he wants to spend time exploring, investigating what his options are, learning what he is good at and discovering what he likes.

For Hiroki's father, his three-stage life had few opportunities to explore and make transitions. For him learning was a first-stage activity, the foundation for what was hoped to be a stable career. Exploring was not only unnecessary, it was also a potentially significant disadvantage. Indeed, his company would have looked suspiciously at him if he dared to break lockstep with his peers. Hiroki realises that these assumptions are changing fast and in their place are emerging multistage lives with more transitions. These transitions will sometimes be chosen (as he hopes his are) and at other times forced (as Ying's next move is).

EXPLORING AND DISCOVERING

We can imagine what Hiroki's choices and options might be by using the schema of possible pathways we described earlier. Recall there are possible selves (shown by the lines); platforms of competencies, skills and networks (shown by the horizontal bars) and stages which illustrate possible changes in direction. In Figure 4.1 we've illustrated a number of possible ways forward for Hiroki. From where he is now in Stage 1, he feels he can either take the path of his father (P2) or he can explore a more unusual path (P1).

The value of options

Hiroki's father wants him to follow in his footsteps and join his company on their management training programme. But Hiroki is more excited about what P1 could look like: he is keen to travel, possibly doing freelance work to support himself, and has an idea for a small business based on his interest in food and fitness. He is not sure where this could lead, but he senses that before he follows any particular path, he wants to discover more about himself. His worry is that if he does not have the courage to strike out on his own path now then, in five or ten years' time, he will have lost the opportunity.

Let's imagine that Hiroki is able to take the bird's-eye perspective on time we illustrated in the last chapter (Figure 3.4).

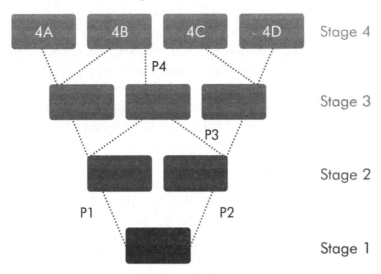

FIGURE 4.1 Hiroki's story

This means he is looking across the whole of his life rather than allowing the present to dominate. From this perspective, because he can look forward, his worry is that by working in his father's firm he will close down the options of possible future selves. Looking at the long life ahead of him, he wants to take time to experiment and see what fits well for him. Yet the challenge for him is that, like many people of his age, Hiroki does not know exactly what he wants. But what he does know is that he has to first properly evaluate whether to follow in his father's footsteps. He wants to discover what his options are and to invest in them; he does not want to simply close them down.

In a sense what Hiroki is experiencing is what Jeffrey Arnett of Clark University, Massachusetts, calls 'emerging adulthood'.[1] Hiroki is no longer a child but has not yet made the commitments that his father had by his age. The twenties used to be a formative decade to establish a family and a career: now it's a time to build the foundational skills and platform for a multistage career and longer life.

What is striking about Hiroki's future paths and the options they contain is how wide and varied they are. Looking forward, careers will inevitably lengthen and job turnover will be faster.

That means the array of possible future selves that Hiroki should consider is much greater than that his father ever faced. That's an exciting prospect, and with the sheer multiplicity of options Hiroki feels no urgency to commit now to a particular path. His father only experienced two transitions: from education to work, and from work to retirement, each in lockstep with his peer group. For Hiroki, breaking lockstep will require much greater experimentation – which is exactly what is causing tension with his father.

Imagine that, as part of path 'P1', Hiroki decides to take time out to learn another language. He goes to Paris for a year, takes a job in a small Japanese restaurant owned by a friend, and immerses himself in learning French. He also registers for an online language course and, with a group of fellow learners from Japan, goes to language classes every morning. He is motivated to learn this new skill and by doing so creates a stronger platform for Stage 2. This widens his options and a creates a variety of possible pathways: one is that, by Stage 4, he is using his language skills to get a job in Paris for a multinational sportswear label that is keen to expand internationally and he then becomes a serial entrepreneur (Stage 4B). Or, taking the same path, P1, he branches out at Stage 2 to use his language skills to build a platform of skills and networks that help him create a small business specialising in importing French cheese and wine to Tokyo (Stage 4A). Of course, at this point in time, Hiroki doesn't know for sure what he wants to be – it's just what he *might* be, and that's precisely why he values exploring. There is real value in doing something, even only for a short while, that keeps his options open and helps him evaluate the enjoyment he might get from each path.

If Hiroki follows his father's path, P2, he creates a different set of options. Joining his father's company does not mean he has to follow in his father's footsteps for the rest of his career; he could decide to branch out later. By joining the corporate training programme he will learn useful skills and broaden his experience. He could then shift to a job in a smaller start-up firm (P3), and over time create a platform of knowledge and financial acumen that would help him start his own company (P4). This would provide an alternative route to becoming a serial entrepreneur in the fourth stage of his life (Stage 4B).

With a longer life ahead, Hiroki can take a number of routes to reach the same stage, but this means he has to think carefully about where he begins. If he takes P1, he will open up a route to a variety of options in the fourth stage of his life (4A and 4B), but not 4C (being a general manager in the Japanese firm he joins at the beginning of his career). Following P2 opens up routes to stages 4B and 4C, but not stage 4A. Crucial will be Hiroki considering what could be lost from each path, the risks involved, and how easy it might be to change paths later. The task is made more complicated as Hiroki has to allow not just for his own current views, but also for how his future self might act.

Hiroki's insistence on the importance of options is puzzling for his father. He has much sympathy for Hiroki's desire to be an entrepreneur but is worried this is a risky choice with a slim chance of success. There are no entrepreneurs in the family or the extended friendship network, so it's hard for Hiroki's father to imagine what Hiroki needs to do or what he could become. What he can't understand is Hiroki's logic in saying that he doesn't want to take the job because he *might* want to do something different later, or that he might take the job for a while and then branch off and do something different. That wasn't the commitment and persistence that led Hiroki's father to succeed in his career. For Hiroki's father the appeal of P2 is its clarity and certainty, yet this is exactly what Hiroki worries about.

LIVING TO LEARN

Tom, Ying, Estelle and Hiroki are beginning to understand that if they want a long career where they can navigate transitions, they will need to keep learning. That could mean learning what it is they want to do next, learning how to reach that goal, as well as learning the skills required. In the three-stage set-up, learning was the *default* in stage one: in a multistage life, it's a *choice*. If they don't seize the opportunity to learn, there is very little institutional force that will make them.

That of course makes living to learn potentially a great deal more rewarding – but also makes it potentially a great deal harder. There are numerous ways that corporations, governments and education systems can really be ingenious about supporting adults to learn – and in Part III we explore what some of these solutions could be. But fundamentally, the onus will be on you.

Think back to your childhood, you maybe remember learning as being easy – that you were living to learn. You went to kindergarten and then to school, your days were filled with learning, and then back home to your parents, who no doubt continued to teach you in their own way. It was a time when learning was your main priority – a natural state. Of course, looking back to your childhood, you've maybe forgotten that learning could be tough. In the words of the sociologist Erving Goffman: 'Almost every activity that the individual easily performs now was at some time for him something that required serious mobilisation of effort. To walk, to cross a road, to utter a complete sentence, to wear long pants, to tie one's own shoes, to add a column of figures – all of these routines that allow the individual unthinking, competent performance were attained through an acquisition process whose early stages were negotiated in a cold sweat.'[2]

Adult learning is very different from these childhood experiences. When Ying or Hiroki set out to learn, though they might want to capture the excitement of learning as a child, their context is very different. When they learnt as children, they were not experiencing a major transition and nor did they have to make big decisions about their commitments. Their childhood learning was a full-time occupation and the primary source of focus and energy. They certainly had some discretion, but for most of the time they followed a well-worn path using tried and tested learning methodologies.

These conditions are rarely in place when adults learn. You could be learning on your own or with a wide variety of people and groups; it's likely your learning is optional – you are choosing to opt in rather than choosing to opt out. Learning will be less about making the strange familiar – and more about making the familiar strange. It is as much about 'unlearning' old habits and ways of thinking as learning new skills and habits. The context could be tough – like Ying you could be learning at the very time when you are under immense pressure as you lose a job or are forced to make a transition. Or like Estelle you could be trying to fit learning into a life already full of other responsibilities. So it's no surprise that learning as an adult is challenging and requires courage and intellectual and emotional effort.

Learning at any age

As Ying in her fifties thinks about what comes next, she knows that she will have to either upskill to learn the more complex parts of a possible accounting job, or reskill to learn the foundations of a completely different job. She is very aware that she will be learning in later life. In doing so, she will inevitably confront others' deeply held stereotypes about age and learning. She is also confronting her own stereotypes and assumptions – she is wondering if she really has the cognitive and emotional capacity to learn the new skills that would support this change in her career.

Aristotle created a vivid description of how the mind atrophies when he compared the brain at birth as hot and pliable, capable of soaking up impressions and this malleability makes learning easy. With age the wax begins to harden and becomes ever more resistant to impressions. That in a sense is the image that Ying has. And whilst it's a compelling image, it turns out to be wrong. Recent studies of the pliability of the brain show it can retain a great deal more 'plasticity' than Aristotle imagined. In other words, Ying can take heart that it is possible to learn at any age.

Neuroscientists capture this notion of plasticity with the concept of neuroplasticity – describing the brain as a flexible muscle which can, if trained and used appropriately, regain abilities that were previously lost. It would be wise for Ying to set herself learning goals and as often as possible to launch herself into activities that are unfamiliar and challenging. As psychologist Denise Park of the University of Texas at Dallas remarks: 'When you are inside your comfort zone you may be outside of the enhancement zone.' In other words, the real reason you can't teach an old dog new tricks is not because the dog has become old, but because it has not continually learnt new tricks.

Ying might also want to consider that not only does the brain retain plasticity, there are forms of intelligence that become more salient with age. Specifically, with age comes the opportunity to develop *crystallised* intelligence. This is the information, knowledge, wisdom and strategies that are accumulated over time and is unlike *fluid* intelligence (which is the ability to process information, memory use and deductive reasoning). There is evidence that, over a lifetime, there seems a constant fluctuation in the relative strength of different mental skills.[3] In your late teens you may be fast at calculating numbers and working out patterns; in your thirties your short-term memory may peak; in your forties and fifties your social understanding is at its highest. Harvard Medical School's Laura Germine and Boston College's Joshua Hartshorne from their research conclude that: 'At any given age, you're getting better at some things, you're getting worse at some other things, and you're at a plateau at some other things. There's probably not one age at which you're peak on most things, much less all of them.'[4]

How to learn as an adult

In 2017 the illustrations used in most Gucci advertisements around the world were created by Ignasi Monreal, a twenty-seven-year-old Spanish artist and illustrator. Using computers and digital tablets, and working fourteen-hour days, Ignasi created more than 150 artworks for Gucci in eight months. Ignasi had made an investment in learning by studying two degrees but this is not where he learnt his digital skills. 'I just learnt from YouTube, it's full of tutorials. I also learnt graphic design there,' he explains. 'I wouldn't necessarily call myself a photographer but I wanted to learn how to use a camera and watched videos until I could use one ... You have to have a lot of patience, but if you have, it's a free education. It's not very curated but if you really want to learn something you can.'[5] What Ignasi did was to shift his learning from degree-based courses towards technologically enabled self-learning with a practical and employment focus.

The provision of adult learning, as we will show in Chapter 7: The Education Agenda, is an industry that is developing fast – creating more content and building more partnerships. Part of this development is an explosion of online material and courses that provides a platform to learning new skills. Ying must be sure to make the most of these new opportunities and, like Ignasi Monreal, have the focus and the courage to learn. Radhika uses the web on a weekly basis to update her current skills and also to branch out to discover more about new skills she might be motivated to learn. Hiroki can learn about French cheese by joining one of the online communities of devoted cheese fans. It's a playground for them to learn in – almost like being a child again.

Yet learning as an adult requires more than logging onto an online course or downloading an app: it's also about creating both a working and home environment that supports you to explore, to learn and to transform.

As neuroscience shows – learning begins with a healthy brain, capable of absorbing and learning new things. It turns out that the brain's capacity to perform higher human activities (such as learning, intuition and creativity) is profoundly impacted by our feelings and emotions.[6] If you are feeling very anxious or stressed then your brain's capacity to change and learn is significantly reduced.[7] This creates a real challenge because in many jobs anxiety and stress is part of the job. In the United Kingdom for example, people miss nearly 70 million workdays a year, and poor mental health (for example, anxiety, depression, and stress-related conditions) is the number one factor contributing to illness-related absence.[8] Indeed the World Health Organisation predicts that depression will be the primary health-related burden worldwide by 2030.[9] If your work makes you anxious (perhaps you feel you've been treated unfairly, or you are worried about losing your job) then you are significantly less likely to learn. This raises the potential paradox of transitions. Transitions, especially those which are forced upon you such as Ying's, are periods when you are most in need of learning – but paradoxically, they are also the time when you may be experiencing the greatest anxiety and pressure.

It is crucial to address this paradox. One way is to ensure you are interested and passionate in what you are learning and so balance the potential anxiety with a sense of purpose. You will learn best, in the words of psychologists, when you are 'intrinsically motivated' – when you find the subject itself fascinating and are curious about it. As Ying considers what she could learn next, she is more likely to make the effort if it's something she is really intrigued by.

Most people learn as they work, and there are ways to expand a job to significantly increase its learning potential: taking the opportunity to work in a different function and location; putting yourself forward for secondments that allow you to take temporary placements in another department; engaging in special projects outside of day-to-day work. Jobs can also be redesigned to bring more autonomy and control over where, when and how you work. As the University of Rochester's Edward Deci and Richard Ryan discovered,[10] having autonomy at work is a precious resource and in fact many people place the value of autonomy beyond other job attributes like pay. There is also the impact on a healthy brain – people with autonomy generally feel less stressed and are less likely to suffer from burnout.

In a longer life, you may want to consider how you use your leisure time – converting it from recreation to re-creation. Already, as a recent survey showed, for almost half of people, the majority of their professional development takes place outside of work – in the evenings and weekends.[11] That motivation and commitment to personal development will be key – whether it's watching TED talks, learning from YouTube, downloading podcasts or taking online courses.

How and what you learn is also shaped by your environment, your physical space and your communities. For Radhika that's an issue – she lacks much of the learning context a company can provide – direction and support, mentoring and sponsorship, guidance and community. Hers is a volatile job, highly sensitive to the rollercoaster of her skills becoming valuable then obsolete in quick succession. It's entirely her responsibility to learn. Not being part of a larger organisation she has to work harder to build her professional reputation and create a network of mentors and role models.

She can take a step in this direction by swapping the isolation of her small apartment with locating in a co-working space, so she alternates time working alone and time with others. She has many options here because in most cities the volume of co-working spaces is rapidly growing. In the US in 2007, there were only about fourteen co-working spaces, and the concept of shared office spaces was unheard of in India. Today there are more than 35,000 globally, with 850 in India alone, providing a workspace for almost 2.2 million people across the world.

Radhika can also ensure her home is a place to learn. In his study of the lives of freelancers, INSEAD's Gianpiero Petriglieri and his co-researchers discovered freelancers typically create places to work that protect them from outside distractions and pressures and help them avoid feeling rootless.[12] He found these spaces had much in common: they felt almost confined, had easy access to the tools of trade, were dedicated to work and typically were left once the daily tasks were completed. Yet despite these commonalities, each workspace was unique, with a location, furniture, supplies, and decorations that reflect the idiosyncrasy of its owner's work.

Radhika has deliberately created a place at home where she can work and learn. Rather than creating a *home* to learn, others will be choosing a *place* to learn. It turns out, as Toronto University's Richard Florida has shown, places differ considerably in terms of their capacity to encourage and facilitate learning, exploring and creativity.[13] Florida began his research by examining places where many patents had been filed, working on the basis that patents were positively correlated with creativity. He discovered what he called 'clusters' – places where creativity and innovation thrive and where there is a rich interchange of knowledge. These locations had much in common. They were anchored in technology – either physical technological institutions or had strong technological infrastructure that allowed easy and efficient communication.

They tended to be places that were tolerant of diversity, so a variety of people – in terms of lifestyle choices, sexual preferences, nationality – felt comfortable congregating there. They were communal – cafes, galleries, and saloons created environments where people were happy to be and could easily find others like them. For freelancers like Radhika, these open, inclusive spaces could play an important role in learning and a sense of identity.

LEARNING TO NAVIGATE TRANSITIONS

The schema of Hiroki's life plan (Figure 4.1) shows greater longevity, multiple stages and more transitions. In forging this path, his focus will be on creating a life of learning that enables him to upskill and reskill as technology redefines what it is to work and the characteristics of a job. Learning how best to navigate these transitions will fast become a crucial skill.

London Business School's Herminia Ibarra shows that although every transition is unique, they all share a number of common factors:[14] they are rarely easy, and for most people they begin with apprehension. As Ibarra observes, no matter how common transitions are, no one has figured out how to avoid the turmoil of change.

In part that is because making a transition, within work or in your personal life, inevitably involves a shift of identity. What you do, how others see you, and how you perceive yourself all change. Ying is beginning to find out what it is to make a transition. She's been given six months by her company to find another job. Her initial thoughts are to take a similar job in another accountancy firm or to become a freelance accountant. But as she thinks about this path she is the first to acknowledge that these are simply variants on her existing identity. She is beginning to wonder whether there are other possible paths that could excite her and provide the promise of unveiling a whole new identity.

As Ying thinks more deeply about the last few years of her role at the accountancy firm, she reflects on how she personally benefited from a work coach who supported her in addressing some of the issues she faced as a manager. Perhaps she could become a coach too? That's a big step and, looking forward, Ying will need to go through several phases if her transition is to be successful. Any transition towards this new skill and identity will inevitably need both a period of exploring and investigation, as well as a later phase of making of commitments.[15] Both of these phases can be unsettling. By exploring, Ying would be putting herself into unusual situations and meeting people she doesn't know, whilst commitments to a future path involve moving away from past areas of competence and confidence.

Investigating

Ying's first efforts are rather insubstantial: glancing through a personal coaching magazine she answers an advertisement for a weekend coaching course. Having not fully explored her options or checked the course out with others, she ends up disappointed. On reflection she realises she'd taken the course precisely because it isn't a real commitment – she is simply pretending to think about becoming a work coach. To really explore she will have to be more proactive.

In conversation with her former coach she explores the idea of volunteering to coach disadvantaged young people. Still working full-time, she is able to fit two coaching sessions into the evenings. It only takes a few weeks for Ying to realise she has a lot to learn. Talking through her experiences with her fellow coaches she finds this new network is giving her useful advice, talking her through her issues, and benchmarking her experiences. She discovers that some have attended a particular evening class and she signs up for it in the next semester. It's a busy time, she is serving out her notice at the accountancy firm while also continuing with her pro bono work. She is still on her old path, while exploring her new path through side projects.

Ying has not yet committed to this new career stage. Over the next four months, as her experience grows and she learns more from her own feedback, she begins to think more deeply about earning her living as a coach. That's a tougher proposition because it means not simply running these as side projects but making a more significant commitment to becoming profession-ally qualified. It also means leaving her identity as an accountant behind and being judged on a whole new set of criteria.

Committing

Within six months Ying has worked out her notice and has registered for a one-year, part-time programme. Her savings pay for her mortgage, but she decides to take some freelance accounting work to pay her everyday expenses. This is not her final destination, but she is prepared to flit between the two paths as she builds the platform for the next part of her life. She joins the loose affiliation of ex-employees from her company and they immediately involve her in a couple of bookkeeping projects they are working on.

Ying excitedly sets about her new life, but soon hits a setback when she receives negative feedback on her coaching skills from a colleague. Things are harder than she imagined, she misses the familiarity of her old job and the camaraderie of her colleagues, and the freelance work she is doing is both pressured and does not really make the most of her skills. What sustains her through this difficult period is the group she is training with. Many are feeling the same, and together they support each other through the course. Studies of how adults learn show how crucial these peer-based 'communities of practice'[16] can be.

Shifting networks

As time goes by, Ying begins to spend more time with her coaching community and less time with her old work colleagues. Her networks are shifting. For Herminia Ibarra this shifting net-work is a sign of all successful transitions. Over the next year when people ask Ying: 'What do you do?' she is less likely to say: 'I'm an accountant' and more likely to say: 'I'm a coach', or perhaps: 'I am learning to be a coach.' Like many people who are making a transition, she has to think again about what is important to her and reflect on her values, priorities and passions. This question of value is really important to her – she makes a lot less money as a coach, but her view is that the satisfaction this job gives her outweighs the monetary loss.

Ying began with a general discomfort about her current situation pushed by losing her job and beginning to feel that coaching might be for her. Then she moved into a transitional period in which she was experimenting – taking side projects, using her extended vacation to go on a weekend course, enrolling in a longer programme and learning how this would work for her. It was only after these small steps that she was prepared to commit, and this involved questioning her values and assumptions.

EXPLORING NEW TRANSITIONS

Clearly every transition entails some form of exploring, and the impact of technology and longevity means there will inevitably be more transitions. But it is not just about more transitions; there will also be new transitions at different stages of life.

The old transitions – from education to first job, or from final job to retirement – were well signposted by social norms developed to ease these transitions. As the three-stage life morphs into a multistage life, these new transitions lack social norms and navigation prompts. So there is a real and pressing need here for social ingenuity to confront the issues that arise as a society, wired for a three-stage life, struggles with the shift to multiple stages.

Hiroki is exploring a new transition as he invests in the options that emerging adulthood requires, rather than making the early commitments that his father made at that age. This will not be the only new transition that Hiroki experiences: we would also expect him to experience a midlife transition as he reinvents and reinvests in order to stay productive. And in later life we should expect him to experience a new transition in his seventies and eighties too as he focuses on positive aging.

A midlife transition: staying productive

In a three-stage life, the thirties and forties were a period when commitments dominated: work was hard and challenging;

families were being raised and elderly parents supported. And whilst this brought much enjoyment, study after study reported a 'happiness curve', where typically happiness declined in this period of life.[17] It's the 'sandwich generation', caught between the demands of children, job responsibilities and aging parents.

These pressures may seem inevitable, especially within the context of a three-stage life, but in fact the term 'midlife crisis' was coined first by the psychologist Elliott Jaques in 1965. Like the emergence of 'teenagers', this is a social construct that became more apparent as life expectancy increased.

As life lengthens even further, it is possible to use the opportunities a multistage life brings to redistribute time and relieve these pressures. In fact, perhaps the notion of a 'midlife crisis' will disappear and be replaced by a 'midlife reinvention'. This reinvention could be financial – accumulating sufficient money so that over the next ten to fifteen years it's possible to step out of work for six months or a year to learn a new skill, spend time with family or engage with the community. It could be exploring – discovering hobbies or subjects of interest that serve as a basis for the next career. It could be reinvigorating – having deep conversations with partners to explore earlier commitments and plan for the future.

Midlife is only a crisis if you can't make the transition to build a new future. Marc Freedman, CEO of the social purpose organisation Encore.org, believes there is not a midlife crisis, but a midlife chasm as society currently lacks the social norms and support to help people make this midlife transition. In response to longer lives, we expect this to change. There are already social pioneers who are leading the way – and as more people are prepared to reinvent themselves, so the education system and the labour market will evolve to support them. Then midlife will be seen not as a crisis, but as an opportunity for reinvention and redirection.

This transition sets the scene for the importance of staying productive for longer. Already more and more older people are working longer. By 2017, roughly 1 in 12 Americans over the age of seventy-five were in paid work. Indeed, since 1998, employment in the US has risen by 22 million – nearly 20 million of whom are people aged over fifty-five.

But it's not going to be that simple. Whilst some people are indeed working for longer, and across the whole labour market, it is still a tough place for older workers. As Figure 4.2 shows, in the US from the age of forty-five people begin to withdraw from paid work; from the age of fifty-four the decline becomes rapid. Some leave out of choice; they feel financially secure and perhaps don't enjoy work and therefore retire before the state pension age. But for many this is not a voluntary action. The driver for some is ill-health, for while many people are living more healthily there still remains an ever-present risk of illness.

For many the decision to leave work is not made by them – it's made by the firm they work for. Often the firm is cost-saving or downsizing and looks first at reducing the number of older (and often more expensive) workers. This is what Ying has discovered. The problem is compounded because once older workers have lost their jobs, they struggle to become re-employed.

FIGURE 4.2 – US labour force participation rate, 2017 (source: Bureau of Labor Statistics)

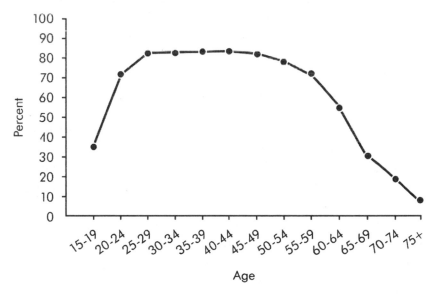

The corporate barriers for older workers are demonstrated persuasively in a study of the impact of age on the chance of being hired.[18] The research team submitted 40,000 fictional CVs to a range of job vacancies, including administrators, caretakers, sales and security. The CVs were identical apart from one detail – the age of the applicant. How firms responded showed clear discrimination: the chance of being called to interview declined from 19 per cent for those aged 29–31; to 15 per cent for those aged 49–51; and down to 12 per cent for those aged 64–6. Another study supported this: those over the age of sixty-two with a college degree had only a 50 per cent chance of becoming re-employed within two years of losing their job; for those between 25–39 it was over 80 per cent.[19] It is no surprise that many older workers eventually give up looking for a job and permanently withdraw from the labour market. As 2017 US data shows, more than a third of those over the age of fifty-five who were looking for a job had been unemployed for more than six months.[20]

As a consequence, a new transition is emerging – positively boosting productivity at an age where previously forward-looking plans were about an impending retirement. This productivity transition could be based on upskilling – making a significant investment in current skills and strengths; or reskilling – finding new ways of maintaining engagement and purposeful activity.

Key to this transition will be making the most of the type of intelligence that becomes salient with age – crystallised intelligence. That means finding jobs that require crystallised intelligence and given that AI finds it easier to mimic the characteristics of fluid intelligence, this will increasingly be a positive in the labour market. This switch to roles or jobs that use crystalline intelligence is exactly what Ying is doing as she transitions into becoming a career coach. In playing to her strengths and experience, she not only thinks she will face the best chances of becoming employed but will also take the greatest pleasure in work that utilises these skills.

Given the corporate barriers that older workers face, another new transition path is opening up – becoming self-employed or starting a business. It's an ageist assumption that only young people start up companies; as Figure 4.3 shows, people who start their own businesses are more likely to be over the age of fifty than under the age of thirty. Even more striking, those over the age of forty are more likely to be setting up a high-growth start-up than younger entrepreneurs.[21]

Some people are choosing to make a complete transition, often with a focus on a greater level of social purpose. That's what the journalist Lucy Kellaway did when, at the age of fifty-eight, she stepped down from her high-profile role as a journalist at the *Financial Times* to retrain as a teacher. Motivated by the idea that 'I can't be the only fifty-something person in the world to want a second career in this most noble of professions', she also established a social enterprise, 'Now Teach'. This supports the transition for people who already

FIGURE 4.3 Starts-ups by age of entrepreneur (source: "Age and High-Growth Entrepreneurship" P.Azoulay, B.Jones, D.Kim, J,Miranda, NBER Working Paper No.24489, April 2018)

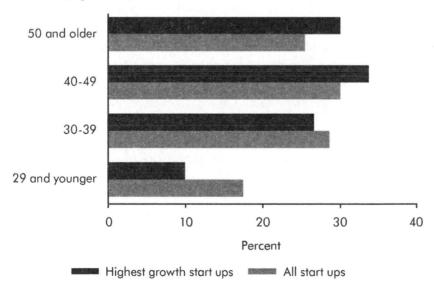

have one successful career and now want to retrain as teachers. Lucy believes there 'is a colossal waste of talent as people who are reaching the end of one successful career want to do something meaningful'.

Now Teach involves a significant transition, shifting from one full-time role to another, but there are a widening variety of ways to engage with social purpose without a full-time commitment (or a salary). If working for longer and a sense of engagement is good for your health and well-being, then finding an 'encore' career to pursue after retirement is an attractive idea. And whilst transitions are difficult, they can be less taxing by parlaying an existing skill acquired in one sector to another sector. Indeed, according to Encore.org, almost 10 per cent of Americans in this age group have already decided to create a new career that combines 'passion and purpose and sometimes a pay check'.

A *later life transition: positive aging*

In a three-stage life, the transition from work to retirement was dramatic. When life expectancy was around seventy-five, this third stage of life involved some years of leisure followed by declining ill health and finally the last transition of all.

For people like Clive in his seventies, the challenging new transition he faces is to make the most of the years he now has ahead of him. Clive has significantly more years of life than his father did at this age. In fact, if we adjust for age inflation then we can calculate that Clive at seventy-one has the same number of years left as his father did when he was aged sixty. This is not straightforward for as more people live for longer, the variance within their age group becomes ever more obvious. As the philosopher Martha Nussbaum notes in her essay on aging thoughtfully, the trouble with stories of aging is that too few show the extent of variety within aging, in terms of health and behaviour.[22]

Some will face this new transition by simply continuing to work – taking on customer-facing roles, supporting customers of their own age, or in occupations where the crystallised intelligence and wisdom they have accumulated is at a premium. In medicine, law, academia and other professions there are social pioneers leading the way, but progress will spread further, across more sectors and covering a wider range of people.

Yet for the majority of people paid work will play a diminishing role in their life, despite the rise in 'unretirement'. With a significant increase in life expectancy, the transitional challenge they face is to be more *forward-looking* and to be prepared to make more investment in their possible future selves. For Nussbaum this forward-thinking is crucial as people age – to be orientated to the present and the future.[23] Her view is that if we look primarily backwards to the past, we are in danger of simply recycling the repetitive roles learnt by memory and of being animated only by the retrospective emotions of nostalgia or regret. Clive would be wise to enjoy the joy of the present and to look forward with hope and anticipation.

This forward-looking transition could mimic the exploration that Hiroki is about to embark on. Clive and his wife could take a 'gap year', exploring the world and meeting up with family or old friends. They would not be alone: over the last fifteen years in the UK for example, it is the over-65s who have accounted for most of the growth in travel spending. It isn't just cruise ships either: in 2018 Airbnb bookings for this age group rose by 66 per cent. This is a time of expansion – expanding activities, expanding networks, expanding competencies, and expanding friendships.

Over time, inevitably, these 'expansion' needs will be met by new societal structures and opportunities. As Nussbaum remarks, if only a small minority of people live long lives, then these survivors are likely to be dispersed and integrated in their family life. But when a majority of people live long lives, then they form a critical mass who are able individually and collectively to explore a much wider set of options.

Clive is already exploring this wider set of options: he has become part of a walking football team (that's football but without any contact or any running). What really appeals to him is both the camaraderie and the competitiveness – he finds the gym a rather solitary experience. He is not alone, still only a few years old, the UK's National Walking Football Association has 434 clubs and rising. Walking football is an example of how the collective actions of social pioneers are creating new social communities to support different lifestyles.

The challenge for Clive is balancing this surprising sense of youthfulness with a growing sense of the need to prepare for the inevitable risks of aging. Clive is very aware that whilst he has more years ahead of him than his father had at his age, he wants these years to be in good health. But he also has to face up to the possibility that this might not be the case. Clive has to manage these later years of life with a delicate balance of forward-looking enthusiasm and mindful preparedness for bad outcomes.

To examine the role that endings play, consider a study by Nobel prize winner Daniel Kahneman and co-authors. Two experimental groups had their hands immersed in cold water (14°C) for 60 seconds. One group then removed their hands after the 60 seconds while a second group kept their hands in the water for a further 30 seconds as the temperature was slowly increased to 15°C. When asked which they preferred, most people preferred the slow increase. Even though they had experienced a longer period of discomfort, the relative improvement at the end made them prefer the longer exposure. In other words, as the authors remark: 'evaluations are often dominated by the discomfort at the worst and at the final moments of episodes'.[24] Part of a good life is a good end. The gerontologist Andrew Elder puts it this way: 'while when you will die and what you will die of are important for most old people, it is how and where they will die that is their main concern'.[25] Endings matter.

As Clive ages he needs to make sure his finances are in order and under someone else's control before he lacks the energy and cognitive capacity to do so. He also needs to consider where he would like to live in the last years of his life, what would be the community he would want to be part of, and how far would he like to be from friends and relatives?

In the USA as more people started to live into their late sixties and seventies, the result was a plethora of retirement villages along the Sunshine Coast of Florida. This was fundamentally based on a three-stage life and so it made sense for the final 'retirement' stage to take place in an age-segregated community. However, as Clive and his cohort are aging better, an interesting shift is occurring. People want to live in cities or towns, to connect to other generations, and to be integrated in a purposeful way within a broader community. Creating intergenerational living in cities is a rising agenda for town planners.

Yet whilst life expectancy has increased, the natural arc of life remains intact. It is this natural arc that Stanford University's Laura Carstensen describes in her theory of 'socioemotional selectivity'.[26] Her observation is that, as people age, they begin to perceive their future as less open-ended and to shift their focus from forward-thinking and future-orientated goals towards activities that are more present-focused. This shift in perspective is less about age and more about a sense of proximity to our end.

This shift helps explain the 'paradox of aging' – that is whilst we fear becoming frail and physically vulnerable, for many people their happiness does not decline as they age and is often higher than for those in midlife. For Carstensen that is because, in this final transition of life, people shift their focus towards more emotionally meaningful activities – they start to reduce their activities and focus their diminishing emotional and physical resources on those relationships that are more likely to create a positive experience. The result is that even as we age and inevitably experience physical and social loss, we can maintain, indeed even improve, our emotional well-being.

This is perhaps the most challenging part of the new transition that Clive is attempting. As a 'young seventy-one-year-old', Clive has more life ahead of him than previous generations. That means he needs to be more forward-looking and more invested in his future. But he also has to be preparing for a later time when his horizons will narrow and his comforts and joys will come in more limited forms.

The challenge of this final transition is made all the more complicated by the sheer diversity in how people age. Clive will have to be aware of and influenced by his own feelings rather than simply taking his steer from others of his own age. As Carstensen points out, this final phase is not a discrete process that happens dramatically at a certain age, rather it is something that builds up over a period of time. However, it isn't something to be feared. In the words of Carstensen, while old age 'has its share of hardships and disappointments ... by the time people get there, they're more attuned to the sweetness of life than to its bitterness'.

YOUR EXPLORING

It would be wise to test your ideas about your own possible future paths through the lens of exploration and learning. Here the emphasis is less about predicting the future and more on understanding the steps necessary to build and explore this future – what would it take to make the plans you have work for you, and how could you maximise the upside?

Make transitions work for you

Take a look at the pathways you are thinking through. Our guess is that they will have embedded within them a number of times when you expect to make a transition – perhaps moving to another type of job, completely changing your career, changing location or even country. Consider them in these ways:

Am I exploring enough? As you look forward to these points of transition, are you setting yourself up to open your narrative and to explore, or are you closing down your options? Are you seeking enough broad advice on what you could be doing? Are you considering your future not just from the perspective of your current self but possible future self?

Will my networks help me modify my plan? Right now you are thinking about this plan for the future as concretely as possible. But inevitably, and optimally, this plan will be changed and modified over time. So consider the extent to which the stages you are imagining provide an opportunity for you to keep your networks dynamic and open and enable you to test and revise your plans.

Ensure every stage is a learning opportunity

The plan you are considering is more likely to succeed if at every stage you are making a significant investment in learning.

How will I feel? Think through each pathway and the stages you are imagining. How does it feel? Will it provide the intrinsic motivation and autonomy that you need to learn? There may be times when you will be under stress and have little autonomy – this could work for one stage, but it will not work for multiple stages.

Will I be learning enough? Take a close look at every stage that you are imagining and sketch out what you believe you will learn. There will be some stages that are 'learning rich', in the sense that you will be significantly broadening your experience and likely to be around people who can inspire you. These will be crucial stages in your life and you would be wise to try to preserve them.

Could I build a platform? Platforms are created when you are able to build specific skills, capabilities and networks that create the foundation for later options. So take a closer look at each of the stages you are considering and decide to what extent they can create a platform. Every stage of your life does not have to be able to do this, but if over time there are few opportunities to do so then realise that you will be limiting your long-term options.

Do I have a place to learn?

The way you create your own space or the location you choose will affect your capacity to learn.

Have I optimised my learning space? At each stage of your life take a look around to establish how you are living. Have you created a space that encourages you to learn?

Where will I live? There may be periods of your life when you need to be living in a 'cluster'; there will be other times when it is not necessary to how you learn. Be aware of the rhythms of these periods.

5

RELATE: CONNECTING DEEPLY

Humans have always gained sustenance from each other, and this capacity to act collectively and build collaboratively has been at the heart of our success.[1] As we live longer lives with more transitions we now have an opportunity to rethink how we form and sustain relationships. The adaptability and flexibility of a multistage life creates many opportunities for us to grow and evolve. But unless we simultaneously deepen and invest in our relationships then, faced with more transitions, there is a real danger of our life fragmenting. We could become adrift from our sense of self and identity.

The central core of our relating is our *families*, our relationships with partners, parents and relatives, potentially spanning many stages of our life. Most of us care deeply about our parents, and we want our children to thrive and achieve a life as good, if not better, than our own. Family structures are morphing into a 'beanpole' rather than pyramid shape, as family members live longer and fewer children are born. With fewer siblings and more generations alive, new responsibilities bring new questions: who, for example, should care for the great grandparents?

Beyond this central core are *close friendships* which can last for decades, and, as the Grant Study described earlier shows, can play a central role in our happiness and life satisfaction. Then there are more transient *networks of relationships*. These networks can span work and leisure and can be crucial to how we learn, providing a source of mentors and role models. The flux created by a multistage life with its many transitions means that keeping contact and investing in relationships built in previous stages needs a great deal more effort, commitment and focus. Radhika works remotely and has to give time to building a work-based community, something that would happen automatically for her friends in more traditional corporate roles.

At the outermost circles of our relationships is our *community and neighbourhood*. There is much enjoyment in being part of a neighbourhood and seeing familiar faces. Then at the widest aperture is *society*, formed by the broad interaction of neighbourhoods and communities. It is this which ultimately and implicitly shapes the broader norms and traditions of our behaviour. But as more of our daily activities take place, virtually and online, so the nature of these casual encounters changes. Indeed, the brilliance of the Internet to match people with similar interests runs the risk of a more segregated society and the dilution of traditional community activities.

Cutting vertically across all these relationships are *generations*. As more generations are alive at any point in time, so their contrasting views of how life should be lived become more apparent. The young have to find new ways of living and with this come growing signs of intergenerational conflict. Avoiding these political rifts will require stepping beyond simple generational caricatures and forging new social and economic partnerships between the young and old.

FAMILIES

Our capacity to thrive and flourish depends in part on our families. When they are nurturing and supportive they can be an important buffer against the vagaries of a fast-changing world. At their best, families pool their time and resources to support each other, providing insurance at times of ill health or unemployment as well as nurturing the young and caring for the old. These attributes become ever more crucial in a world characterised by longer lives, technological disruption and fluctuating multistage careers.

Whilst there are many similarities in the basic role of the family, there are important cultural and social differences between

108

countries. Radhika might work full-time in India, but with only 30 per cent of Indian women performing paid work she is very much a minority. Madoka is striving for a balanced partnership with her boyfriend Hiroki, but currently most Japanese men do not view childcare as a key part of their role.

These national differences are not static and are changing in response to the cultural and social pressures created, in part, by technology and longevity. In Japan, for example, there is much current debate about the role of women in society, the outcome of which will shape the choices Hiroki and Madoka make about how to bring up their family. That's important because the nature of families is changing alongside the shift to longer multistage lives. If families are to provide cohesiveness in our relationships and the resource sharing that helps sustain and insure us over the life course, we desperately need social ingenuity and social pioneering to reimagine family roles and responsibilities.

Marrying later

As life lengthens, so people are delaying making commitments, and this is no more apparent than in marriage. In 1890, the median age of marriage for an American women was twenty-two; it's now around twenty-eight.[2] Very few of Hiroki and Madoka's friends were married before the age of thirty. They are not alone in delaying this choice: people in Sweden marry latest (thirty-seven for men and thirty-four for women), compared to much earlier in India (twenty-three for men and nineteen for women).

Others are choosing not to marry. In the 1970s in Japan, being unmarried was rare, only 1 in 50 men over the age of fifty was unmarried, now it's 1 in 4. For women it was 1 in 33, and now it's 1 in 7.[3] When Radhika and Madoka talk to their girlfriends, there is much debate about the merits of marriage. Radhika wants to focus on her career, she doesn't want the commitment of a more stable relationship. In part this reflects the increasing economic independence of women, which makes the financial benefits of marriage less appealing. It's also a result of techno-logical ingenuity. Radhika can use microwaves, freezers and food-delivery services, to name a few, to make life easier whilst she earns her living working. In fact, there is evidence that as people earn more, they want more privacy and independence.

Given these shifts, it's no surprise there's a growing social narrative to support a single life as a positive choice. In her TED talk, the social psychologist Bella DePaulo argues that whilst marriage is still idealised as the social norm, single women are pioneering and pushing back against conventional expectations and constraints. Her view is that single people are creating twenty-first-century connections and intimacies which go beyond the old nuclear family model,[4] and unlike common stereotypes, are highly connected to their friends and relatives. They don't seem to suffer from the insular nature and shrinking networks that some research has shown in cohabiting or married couples.

The increase is not just in single adult households, but also in single-parent families. Looking back to the seventeenth and eighteenth century, this was not unusual: between half and a third of families were headed by a single parent due to high adult mortality. As people lived longer this changed and ever more households had two surviving parents. The proportion of single-parent families has, however, begun to rise again: in part because the divorce rates of married couples has increased; and in part because more people choose to cohabit and this carries a higher risk of separation than marriage. In Africa, Latin America and the Caribbean, around 30 per cent of families are headed by a single parent, compared to 20 per cent in Europe, 28 per cent in the US and around 13 per cent in Asia. In all cases, such households are predominantly headed by a woman.

Life in these single families can be tough, as Estelle has found. Single-parent households are the most economically vulnerable, with children twice as likely to live in poverty than those living in two-parent households. Estelle is certainly happy to no longer live with her husband, but the minimal financial support she receives from him means she has to work and be sole carer for her children. To do this she is very reliant on the support of her relatives, especially the older generation, as well as her friends. Estelle is very grateful for the support of her parents and aunts and uncles, but she is also conscious of just how vulnerable she is if she becomes ill or loses her job. These arrangements help support her whilst she works, but she's less sure if her extended family have the resources to help her through the more significant transitions a multistage life demands.

Choosing fewer children, inheriting more older relatives

People are marrying later and having children later. The average age for a first child in Japan is thirty-one, compared to twenty-seven in the US. In the UK you are now more likely as a woman to have a child in your forties than if you are under the age of twenty.

Women are also having fewer children – or indeed no children. Looking back to the 1940s, in the developed countries this was rare – only about 10 per cent of adults over the age of forty did not have children, it's now between 15–20 per cent. In Japan, of those women born in 1953 (now in their sixties) 10 per cent did not have children, for those born in 1970 (now in their forties) it is 1 in 4. In India, Radhika is wondering whether to have children; her friends remind her of the cost and she sees how tough it can be to combine careers and family. She also wonders with the advances in fertility treatment whether she can postpone this decision into her forties. For her grandparents in rural India, children were crucial both for agricultural work and a means of financial support in their old age. But as economists Shelly Lundberg and Robert Pollak remark: 'As the narrowly economic motives for childbearing and childrearing decline in importance, from the parents' standpoint, children look less like investments and more like expensive consumer durables.'[5]

This means that, though Radhika, Hiroki and Madoka live in different countries, they will probably spend their twenties considering their options and developing their platform of skills and networks. They are unlikely to be focusing on having children or embarking on the traditional paths of adulthood. They are entering a new stage of life, a stage that often means they will remain in the family home. Tom's adult son is living with him and across the US for the first time in 130 years, 'living at home' is now the dominant arrangement for people between the ages of 18–34.

As a result of having fewer children later in life and of living longer, Hiroki and Madoka will spend *proportionately* less of their total lifetime caring for children. So they have more time to develop their careers and engage in leisure activities. However, at the same time, they will be living in a family with more generations. Indeed by 2030 it is estimated that over 70 per cent of American eight-year-olds will have a living *great-grandparent.*[6]

This has profound implications for Hiroki and Madoka's caring activities. They will spend less time caring for their own children, but proportionally more time caring for their parents, grandparents and great-grandparents. These 'longer' families, often blended through divorce and remarriage, raise interesting questions about familial responsibilities. Take Tom, whose father remarried later in life and moved to Florida before he passed away three years ago. Tom doesn't know his now widowed stepmother that well. He's heard that she has moved from the house she shared with his father and is now living on her own, but he hasn't been to see her since his father's funeral. What are Tom's obligations, if any, to her?

With declining fertility rates, there will also be a rising proportion of older people with few relatives to visit or care for them. This reduces the ability of the family to fulfil its traditional role of caring for older relatives and is an area ripe for social ingenuity. People are already pioneering solutions by creating alternative 'families'. Take for example a group of seven women in Guangzhou, China. In their thirties they bought a house together with the aim of it being their home throughout their lives.[7] As family structures can no longer support the insurance and pooling needs of individuals, so alternative household structures will inevitably be created.

Working Families

More women are in paid work, with the demands of housework reduced by a raft of household devices, and, with improvements

112

in contraceptives, exercising choice about when to have children and how many to have. In 1920, only 1 in 5 American and 1 in 3 British women were occupied in paid work; now it's 3 in 5, and in Iceland it is nearly 4 in 5. With ever more domestic technological ingenuity, the continuing trend for women to have fewer children and to marry later, and the possibility of multistage longer working careers, we expect this proportion to increase yet further across the world.

When Madoka and Hiroki talk about the life they would like together, they agree on two principles: to pursue interesting and purposeful work; and to both take an active role in their family. From her perspective, Madoka knows she is unlikely to be able to have a career and have children unless Hiroki takes an active parenting role. For Hiroki his commitment is not simply about Madoka; he wants to be a more engaged father than his own. So the task they face is to forge a relationship that supports both of them in their careers, whilst giving them the flexibility to truly co-parent. In other words, they want a relationship where their roles are not predetermined by their gender.

The implication is that Madoka's life will be very different from her mother's, who left her office job as soon as she was married and stayed at home to care for her children. The same was true in many Western societies until around 1950. Indeed, the 'marriage bar' was a widespread barrier and a formal or informal restriction that forced women once they married to leave their job. The view was that women did not need to work because they were financially supported by their husband, and if they did work they were taking away jobs from men who needed them to finance their family. Once children were grown up, women did return to the workforce, often in a part-time role – as was the case with Madoka's mother. This working pattern produced the clear 'M' shape in the left-hand side of Figure 5.1.

If you consider the most recent cohorts of younger Japanese women, they look a great deal more like their American counterparts. Indeed, Japan's younger women are now more likely to work full-time than their American counterparts – never

113

FIGURE 5.1 Japanese and American women's labour force participation by birth cohort and age group[8]

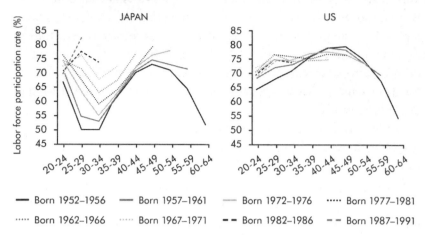

— Born 1952–1956   — Born 1957–1961   — Born 1972–1976   ····· Born 1977–1981

····· Born 1962–1966   ····· Born 1967–1971   – – Born 1982–1986   – – Born 1987–1991

have so many Japanese women of any age wanted to be at work. Madoka, unlike her mother, is determined to maintain her career.

This will not be easy: corporate Japan's working practices are inflexible, and whilst many more women are working, the *type* of work they do differs in important ways from men. Whilst 75 per cent of women between the ages of 22–65 work, about a quarter of these women are working part-time (compared to 10 per cent of men). As a consequence, they earn less, have a lower pension and are less likely to be promoted. This is not purely a Japanese phenomenon. Across the OECD countries, whilst almost half of workers are women, they occupy less than 30 per cent of managerial jobs and in Japan only 10 per cent of senior jobs are held by women. In other words, women tend to have jobs rather than careers.

This has an impact across all features of the labour market. In the OECD, women on average earn 14 per cent less than men. Indeed, even if a woman is more educated than her partner, she still only has a 36 per cent chance of earning more than him. This is exacerbated by the sectors women work in: they are more likely to work in lower-paying sectors such as health, education and personal services and not the higher-paying and more male-dominated sectors such as finance, banking and insurance.

The gender pay gap has real implications for young couples and the roles they negotiate and play within the family. If the assumption is that Madoka will earn less than her husband across her career, then she is under financial pressure to put Hiroki's career ahead of hers. Only when there is an assumption that women and men will earn the same across their lifetime can we expect it to become automatic for both partners to consider taking equal share of the economic and caring roles within the family.

There is evidence that the picture is changing, albeit slowly, and as Alison Wolf of King's College, London, has shown, the pay gap is currently smallest for the most educated women.[9] She has observed that women graduates typically have fewer children (as well as often not marrying or having children), and take less time off when they have children. In other words, if the trajectory of women in the workplace mirrors more closely that of men, they are more likely to receive equal pay.

A changing economic role for women in the family is also emerging in lower income households. The proportion of men in paid work is falling so that today in Australia, France, and Germany around 1 in 10 men between the ages of 25–64 are not in paid work; in the US it's 1 in 8. That might seem odd because unemployment is currently very low in the US, but the actual level of male employment is now below what it was during the Great Depression.[10] One possibility is that men are choosing to take a caring role in their family. But this does not seem to be the case, for whilst a growing proportion of men look after their children, it is a very small proportion and does not account for much of the shift. A more likely reason is the fall in demand for low-skilled 'masculine' jobs. In the words of Brookings Institute's David Wessel: 'it's no longer possible to get a good job with just a strong back and a good attitude'.[11] As working careers extend and technology advances, low-educated households are more likely to be economically headed by a working woman rather than a man, especially as the couple ages.

115

These shifts in family social norms will create more variety in the forms that households can take and therefore wider options for people to exercise choice. This fundamentally changes the traditional ideal of a marriage and opens up space for social pioneers – creating new forms of partnerships and novel ways of living together and bringing up children.

But that does not take away from the fact that the essence of being human is to love and to be loved. We expect that what will come in the place of traditional marriage is not less, but more interest in building committed relationships. This will require a heightened level of *interdependence* – both because of the sheer diversity of possible arrangements as well as the complexity of coordinating multistage lives. It will also require more conversations and negotiations because in the absence of social norms each couple will have to find their own way of making things work.

Facing up to choices

This novelty, diversity and complexity makes it hard for Madoka, Hiroki and Radhika to evaluate the likely outcomes of choices they make in how to live their life. There will be times when a situation arises which is both highly consequential and highly problematic, a moment when the array of 'possible selves' begins to change and they are faced with consequential actions that past experience or tradition is unlikely to give much of a steer. How Radhika, Madoka and Hiroki chose or choose their life partner is one of these moments.

Radhika is single and doesn't want to marry until she is in her thirties – she imagines herself then in a partnership with children and pursuing interesting work. Given this image of her possible future self, are there any choices that Radhika should be making now that will increase the likelihood that she will achieve this? Her mother's life was very different from hers – but there are still aspects of the past that could inform her decisions.

116

We know something of these past decisions from a study by Kathleen Gerson of New York University of the choices a group of American women made in the 1970s and the subsequent consequences of these choices which are still being manifested today.[12]

A number of factors and choices they made then shaped their current circumstances. The first was *timing*: it turned out that the age they married and had children impacted on whether they went on to have a career. Those women who had a career were less likely to marry, and if they married, they did this late. Of the working women, 40 per cent did not have children, and those women who did rarely had more than three. What also shaped their future was the *type of person* they married; those who married supportive partners were more likely to continue to work; those whose partners opposed their work quickly dropped out of work. Their *education* also shaped their subsequent life: those with a college or postgraduate degree were more likely to continue to work. And fate also played a hand. If they or a near relative, such as their mother or father, suffered from extended *ill health* they were more likely to drop out of work.

This illustrates the impact of the choices women made in the 1970s. Perhaps the impact of timing, choice of partner and investment in education will be different for today's twenty-year-olds? Certainly the scope of options Radhika faces is wider – she has the option of freelance work and the flexibility this brings, and probably a wider choice of partners. But it would be wise for her to carefully think through these early choices.

A shared narrative

Hiroki and Madoka are talking seriously about sharing the family roles. As they do so what is clear to them both is an overwhelming sense of interdependence. Of course, their parents also shared an interdependence through the specialised tasks of the family – fathers taking care of financial matters and mothers raising the family. One alone was incomplete and neither acted

117

independently. However, the interdependence required by Hiroki and Madoka is even more interlinked and profound.

As social pioneers they have to invent a new form of partnership that has an opportunity for career + career rather than career + job or career + carer. There are many options they can take to achieve their joint career goals and successfully raise a family. Yet without *conscious interdependence* the momentum of greater choice and flexibility could result in the disintegration and fragmentation of their family.

It could be that their relationship takes on the form described by the sociologist Anthony Giddens as *pure* in the sense they don't look to the past for guidelines but rather look to the future. They are 'free-floating', no longer anchored in the external conditions of social or economic life such as the division of labour or based on the rearing of children. So this form of new relationship becomes a creation of two people, rather than a reflection of broader social custom. This is not a straightforward option for Madoka and Hiroki. It will not be possible for them to 'coast along' in ways that might have worked in traditional partnerships. They will have to talk extensively with each other about what they want and what they desire, creating a shared narrative of what is as well as what could be possible. They will need to be 'reflexive':[13] thinking and discussing deeply what is important to them, agreeing what they want, and the commitments they are prepared to make. They will have to make their choices according to what they need and desire, and also what they see happening around them.

They will not be alone. As Judith Stacey of New York University has shown,[14] around the world people are actively constructing new forms of family relationships, and these reconstructions are not trivial. Hiroki and Madoka may take heart from Stacey's view that what is happening is no less than a massive process of experimentation and reconstruction of the model of what a partnership should and could be. This is taking place at a time of under-institutionalisation, where current institutional norms have not yet caught up with fast-changing human desires.

This means Madoka and Hiroki will potentially be more able to create the family structures they desire as under-institutionalisation provides the space for them to decide what they want and to act upon that desire.[15] They can make their choices on the basis of their curiosity, on what they see around them, and on their own judgements about the future.

To consider what this new pathway could look like, let us return to the schema we created for the possible selves and pathways for Hiroki (Figure 4.1). We imagined he could stay on the path his father has imagined for him or take another path which opens up his options to travel and to possibly build a business. But notice that this was a single narrative. At no time during that exploration of his possible paths did we take into consideration that he would be with Madoka and that she may also want a career. In other words, we had imagined his possible paths as independent rather than interdependent. We considered a solo narrative but not a shared narrative.

So let's now overlay this interdependence. We can imagine that both Madoka and Hiroki decide to take their own working pathways, both deciding to join local companies. In Figure 5.2 we show this as paths P1 and P2. Then in their early thirties (Stage

FIGURE 5.2 Madoka and Hiroki's story

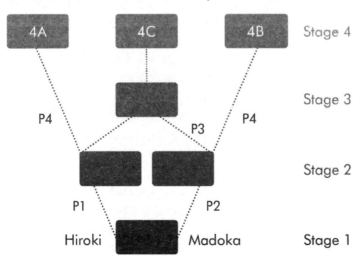

119

2), they both decide to continue to work full-time, but together take six months out to travel. They are taking path P4 which will lead them to their own unique Stage 4. They have decided to not have children yet and instead concentrate on their careers. One of their decision criteria was the likely speed of change in Japanese corporations. Their belief is that Japanese corporations will be slow at introducing flexible work for both men and women. The current gender gap will inevitably impact Madoka's career if she decides to focus on her family rather than her career.

Who looks after the children?

There are other paths they could take. One possibility is that in their thirties, at Stage 2, they decide to have a family. One of their options is that Madoka quickly returns to full-time work to pursue her career, with Hiroki switching roles and taking primary responsibility for childcare. There is some evidence that the number of stay-at-home dads has increased in some countries, though the actual proportion is still remarkably low.[16] But we could imagine that as the gender pay gaps narrow and the educational advantage of women is better reflected in the proportion of senior roles they occupy, so more dads will take the caring role.

Another option, preferred by Hiroki, is that they both work and take an equal share in raising the family. Parents in countries such as Denmark and Sweden are already taking this option and working fathers are almost as engaged in the home as working mothers.[17] But outside of these countries the practice is not widespread and it will certainly take much social ingenuity and changes in both social customs and economic fundamentals to support it. The need to do so will become doubly important as the number of older family members increases and the caring needs of the family extend across the generations.

Hiroki would like to spend more time with his children than his father was able to. He is not alone. In a research study by Robin Ely and her colleagues at Harvard Business School, a group of educated men were asked whether they anticipated a more equal share of childcare in the future. When the researchers asked men aged 49–67, only 16 per cent anticipated this would be the case. For those aged 33–48 it was 22 per cent; while for those aged 18–32 over a third anticipated that they would take equal share of childcare.[18]

This aspiration to be more actively involved in childcare will need major changes in corporate practices. In Japan, where the birth rate has declined so rapidly, the hope for Madoka and Hiroki is that a shortage of workers will force firms to promise greater flexibility in order to attract young recruits. Governments will also need to support these changes. Indeed, in Prime Minister Abe's 'Japan Revitalisation Strategy' the issue of 'womanomics' has been central. This strategy involves a series of policies aimed at increasing the number of women in senior leadership positions, improving childcare options, encouraging men to be more active parents, and enabling working practices that offer a better work–life balance. The challenge will be whether these government policies will have traction in the corporate and family culture of Japan.

Madoka and Hiroki have to take a bet on this future. They are optimistic about change and on the basis of this belief plan to take P3. It is a path of greater interdependence where they will both continue to work but take flexible options in order to jointly care for their children. As a consequence, at Stage 4 they arrive together at path 4C. The option to work flexibly and take joint care of their children has risks – perhaps corporate practice will not change and there is a career and financial penalty to flexible working. And if the gender pay gap persists, then the financial pressure will probably lead to Madoka changing her ambitions and for them to move to a career + job or career + carer model.

A secure base and joint commitments

Madoka and Hiroki are part of a cohort of social pioneers trying to make a career + career model work. This is a cohort that is being watched with interest by researchers such as Jennifer Petriglieri, from INSEAD.[19] Her observation is that these negotiated, commitment-rich partnerships can enable each partner to develop a deeper and broader sense of themselves and their identity. Because both are anchored in meaningful work, they can provide mutual support to each other and that helps build stronger professional identities. The strength of the relationship has the potential to create a 'secure base', where each provides support and encouragement to the other.

This 'secure base' could in the long run be crucial to Madoka and Hiroki. It is very possible that their work and the workplace will become increasingly short-term, and the tasks they do more fragmented, instrumental and 'unbundled'. Given this, their partnership has the potential to be a crucial social institution that compensates for this lack of traditional anchoring and organisational identity. Moreover, this 'secure base' could act as a platform that enables them both to take risks and make transitions. Indeed, this interdependency could enable both of them to accrue a range of resources that neither could have accrued alone. So, rather than a 'win-lose' experience, it becomes a 'win-win'. They achieve more and grow more together than they could have independently. This secure base could be a real asset to them across their lives, enabling them to smooth out the time and financial pressures of multistage and non-linear careers. They have more chance of becoming a 'see-saw' couple, alternating the rhythms across their lives.

Pivotal to their partnership will be making commitments. These commitments frame and acknowledge the risks each is taking. Each person is sacrificing some of their independent future options in favour of a shared future of interdependence. Traditional relationships are of course also based on commitments; Madoka's mother committed to look after the children, while her father committed to support the family financially. This made it relatively straightforward since their commitments were bolstered and supported by social norms and choices. They were also based on fewer options and sequences than the multistage life offers. So while the essence of what makes for a good relationship remains the same, the absence of external guides in the form of social norms requires Madoka and Hiroki to invest all the more in making commitments that will arise from those ongoing conversations and continual communication that characterise their relationship.

To do this they will crucially need to build and maintain mutual trust. This mutual trust cannot be taken for granted and, like other aspects of their relationship, it has to be worked on. They will need to be trusting and trustworthy – believing they can rely on what the other says and does – taking time each day to listen to each other, seriously discussing substantial issues, and sticking with issues until they are resolved.

As Stanford economist Myra Strober remarks in her autobiography based on her research and experience: 'Two people can be in a sustained and nourishing relationship with satisfying careers for both, but *only* if both are fully committed to going that route. If both you and your partner *are* committed, you will find a way to make it work.'[20]

GENERATIONS

As we live longer there are inevitably more generations alive at any point in time. At their best, these intergenerational relations provide resources, support and nurturing for each other, as is the case in Estelle's family. When they work well, each generation feels they are understood and treated fairly.

However, there is a feeling that intergenerational relationships, whilst potentially harmonious within families, are becoming tense across generations. This tension is playing out in politics. Take the UK, where the vote to leave the European Union could be divided by age: 61 per cent of men aged 18–24 voted to stay in the EU; exactly the same proportion of men aged 50–64 voted to leave. In the US, voting patterns are also becoming more marked by age. Indeed Stanford historian Niall Ferguson believes that 'a generational division is growing in American politics that could prove more important than the cleavages of race and class'.[21]

There is no doubt that a healthy human society as well as a happy family is built in part on good intergenerational relationships. But it seems that these are coming under pressure as technological ingenuity is rapidly changing jobs and careers, whilst longevity is changing the balance between young and old.

Generational equity: are the young worse off than the old?

At the dawn of the French Revolution, the English poet William Wordsworth wrote: 'Bliss was it in that dawn to be alive./ But to be young was very heaven.'[22] At the dawn of a revolution spurred by AI and longer lives, the same cannot be easily said by today's young.

For their parents or grandparents, certainly in the developed world, a three-stage life was sufficient to support a family, a house and a pension. For the young this is an unlikely prospect. They will not experience a lifelong career in the same role or even the same sector and need now to plan for a sixty-year career. And whilst for their parents' generation a university qualification offered a failsafe for a career and a good salary, this is unlikely to be their experience. In many countries the young are finding it harder to get jobs and to get on the initial rung of the career ladder; they can anticipate more career disruption, and cannot rely on their initial education to propel them through their entire career. For older generations the three-stage life could provide a steady career and financial stability; for the young the future appears just one long hustle.

There is also the vexing question of rising house prices. In major cities these are working against the young and leading to sharp falls in the rate of home ownership. In the UK the decline is dramatic: thirty-year-olds are now only half as likely to own a house compared to those currently in their sixties and seventies.[23] The same is true in Australia and the US. As a consequence, the young are a generation who will reach their forties with significantly less wealth than past generations.

To compound matters, society is standing behind the health and pension commitments made to earlier generations. A three-stage life was essentially designed for a life expectancy of seventy years; it is now being stretched to eighty-five years and being financed in part by the working young, who will receive few if any of the same future benefits. In 1936 when Franklin D. Roosevelt accepted the Democratic nomination for president he remarked: 'To some generations much is given. Of others much is expected.' That has an ominous sound to the young in many countries. In Japan a new word – *rougai* – is used to refer to the harm or inconveniences, big or small, that are inflicted on the young by a growing elderly population.[24]

These multiple pressures are leading to a belief in some countries that the young will be worse off in the future than their parents were.[25] In Japan, 38 per cent of people believe their children will be worse off (compared to 28 per cent who think they will be better off); in France it is 71 per cent (compared with only 10 per cent who expect an improvement). This isn't a global phenomenon, and parents in fast-growing economies, such as India or China, are more positive. In these countries, economic growth of between 5–7 per cent per annum is leading to income doubling every 10–14 years. As a result, it is no surprise that in India 65 per cent of people think the young will be better off; in China it's 78 per cent.

Of course not all is bleak for the young. If we consider issues such as sexual identity and the progress made by the LGBT agenda, the young are in many ways better off than previous generations. And improvements in life expectancy, both achieved and potentially, in the future, mean the young should also benefit from longer lifespans. One recent study[26] suggests that the extra three years of life expectancy that citizens of France benefit from, compared to the US, is worth the equivalent of 16 per cent of an individual's annual consumption. On that basis, income would need to fall a lot compared to that of their parents, for today's young not to be better off overall if life expectancy continues to increase.

We believe that at the heart of this intergenerational conflict is the unsustainability of the three-stage life. The growing gap between technological and social ingenuity means that the three-stage life is no longer viable and the young need a new chart to map their future life that provides economic prosperity and a platform to flourish as humans.

However, whilst the younger you are the more substantial the changes you will need to make in establishing a new long life, whatever your age, changes have to be made. Everyone is embarking on a process of change. The nature of change may differ across generations, but they do not have to compete with each other to fulfil these needs. What is needed are political institutions that help different ages work together in life rather than create intergenerational conflict.

Take for example the approach in Japan of Future Design.[27] This experiment, conducted in 2015 in the town of Yahaba, asked citizens to draw up a long-term vision for the town until 2060. They were split into two groups: one was asked to imagine and represent the views of the current generation; the other the views of those who would be active in 2060. Inevitably those who were representing future generations demanded a tougher line on current difficult issues, while those who focused on the present situation were more accommodating. What was fascinating was that the experiment did indeed lead to different outcomes, but perhaps more importantly, it changed the mindset of those citizens who were asked to represent future generations. In areas such as climate change the need for such an approach is especially acute.

Generational labels: are the generations really different?

The view of a broader intergenerational conflict is fed in part by generational labels. These labels are a staple of media and business analysis, with headlines such as 'Managing with five generations in the workforce', 'Ten things millennials like' and of course, 'Ten things millennials don't like'. Seemingly every day a newspaper article will report that 'Millennials/baby boomers are having more/less sex', or 'eating more avocados'.

These labels probably began with Gertrude Stein's creation of the term the 'Lost Generation' for people born between 1883–1900. Then came the 'Greatest Generation' (in the US the 'GI Generation'), born between 1901–24, and the 'Silent Generation' (1925–42). The most famous label of all is the 'baby boomers', born between 1943–64, who have transformed every stage of life they passed through. Following them, born between 1965–79, are what Douglas Coupland named 'Generation X', and then the 'millennials' (1980–2000) sometimes referred to as 'Generation Y', who are now the largest generation in the US and by 2020 will be 50 per cent of the global population. More recently comes 'Generation Z' (2001–13) or the 'iGeneration'. Who comes next? A fixed name hasn't yet been settled on a group who are still under ten, but the phrase 'Generation Alpha' seems to be heading the pack.

These generational labels are troubling in part because they seem so arbitrary in their dates and labelling. Within a family, the concept of a 'generation' is well defined. But it is not so clear for a whole society. Within your family, your father and mother clearly belong to a previous generation. But the dividing point between generations is not age, but rather the status in the family tree. That is different in a society where generations are defined by their year of birth. That leads to the possibility that you may have an uncle who is a baby boomer and an aunt who is Generation X. So whilst in a family the meaning of a generation is clear, at the level of a society it is more arbitrary.

Another troubling feature of generational labels is their modernity. Before the late nineteenth century there was no consciousness of a 'generation' – or if there was, it wasn't felt necessary to comment on it or coin a name tag for it. People were just young or old. While Shakespeare referred to the seven ages of man, he didn't feel the need to resort to generational labels. However, as Neil Howe and William Strauss remark, since 'the 1920s there hasn't been a 20 to 25 year cohort that hasn't come of age without at least one determined attempt to name it'.[28] What's interesting is that generational labels emerged at about the same time as the formation of a three-stage life. It was the concept of three stages that resulted in the pronounced institutional segregation of society by age: educational institutions contained people aged twenty-one or under; working institutions people up to the age of sixty-five; and with the advent of retirement, new communities for the elderly were established.

The nature of this institutional age segregation is vividly illustrated by an incident in 1996 in the ironically named Youngtown, a suburb of Phoenix, Arizona. At that time sixteen-year-old Chaz Cope wanted to live with his grandparents in order to avoid his stepfather. However, the retirement community of Youngtown required every household to have at least one resident over the age of fifty-five, and, importantly for Chaz, children under the age of eighteen were banned from staying more than ninety days. The case became a legal clash between the city council, the state attorney, the citizens of Youngtown, and Chaz's grandparents. During the clash the police even took to enforcing this segregation by following school buses to ensure no children were dropped off.

What is interesting is that over time, as society has become ever more age segregated, the reliance on generational labels has increased. The temptation is to conclude that as people spend less time with people outside of their age group, they know them less and therefore resort to generational stereotypes to fill in their lack of knowledge and insight.

Are generational labels useful?

In deciding whether these labels are a help or hindrance to intergenerational relationships, it is useful to consider whether they reflect significant empirical differences. This in turn requires defining what a generation is from the viewpoint of society. The classic definition is that of German sociologist Karl Mannheim: a group of the same age sharing an era in history.[29] In other words, a generation is defined by an age-specific perspective to the zeitgeist. The appeal of the idea of belonging to a generation is captured in Martin Heidegger's remark that 'the inescapable fate of living in and with one's generation completes the full drama of individual human existence'.

However, as Mannheim himself noted, not every age needs to define a generation. If the world of the twenty-first century is effectively the same as the twentieth century, then the context in which we live remains unchanged and social norms and values persist. In these circumstances there is no need to identify generations and a simple focus on young or the old is sufficient. It is therefore *social change* that defines a new generation as they question accepted wisdom, behave in their unique way in response to new challenges, and develop their own values and perspectives. They are, in a sense, the battalions engaged at the front line of social ingenuity. From this perspective, the various boundary dates used to define generations are bookends of specific historical periods of change. This also explains why so many of the more recent generational labels are based around attitudes towards technology. If technology has been changing rapidly, we would expect an increased turnover in generational labels.

However, for generational labels to be powerful these historical changes need to be both sharply defined and play a dominant role in explaining differences in individual behaviour. If change happens slowly and spreads out over years, then the sharp boundaries of generational labels will mislead. The generational label for Madoka and Radhika is 'millennials', and clearly they were brought up in a different technological world than Tom and Ying, let alone Clive. That undoubtedly helps provide insights into differences in behaviour between these groups. However, for these generational labels to be powerful they must account for both a substantial part of the differences between Madoka/Radhika compared with Tom/Ying as well as predict a great deal of similarity in how Madoka and Radhika or Tom and Ying will behave.

In this light it is perhaps not surprising that meta-analysis of studies which have explored the potential variance between generations shows very few significant differences. In fact, the variation in values and behaviours within a cohort of millennials, for example, is much greater than the differences between the average millennial and the average baby boomer.[30] In other words, people are just people. Both of us like avocados on toast, but that doesn't make us millennials.

The danger is that generational labels could be nothing more than a demographic version of astrology, using arbitrary dates to form judgements about individual personality and needs. The resulting generalities and exaggerated differences can be pernicious, especially in the corporate world. One of the most commonplace statements we hear in a business-school setting about millennials is they want meaningful, flexible and purposeful work. But, step back for a moment – surely that's something people of all ages want? This was clear when we analysed the thousands of people who completed the short diagnostic test on the website for our last book, *The 100-Year Life*. In the diagnostic we asked people to rate various aspects of their life and where they focused their attention. We were struck by how little these responses differed by age. Both young and old invested in their skills, were positive and excited about work, and strived to keep fit.[31]

The problem of generational labels, in the words of the German art historian Wilhelm Pinder, is they emphasise 'the non-contemporaneity of the contemporaneous'. Everyone is responding to the changes in technology and longevity. Explaining this simply through the lens of generational labels removes their shared contemporary context and focuses instead on their ages. This is clearly the case in the narratives about technology. Most baby boomers grew up in an environment without smartphones or social media and that is different from their grandchildren who are 'tech savvy' and natural users of technology. But that doesn't mean that baby boomers *cannot learn*; it is just that they *have to learn*.

And they are learning. Even as recently as 2012, only 40 per cent of US baby boomers used social media compared to 81 per cent of millennials. By 2018 the use of social media amongst millennials barely increased; in baby boomers it has risen to 57 per cent.[32] Technology is transforming how everyone lives and communicates and its impact isn't restricted to groups of a particular age.

None of this is to deny that careful empirical analysis based around generational labels can provide insights. These will be invaluable if we are to work across generations to redesign the map of life in a way that works not just for Clive, Tom and Ying, but also for Madoka, Hiroki and Radhika. However, too often these generational labels are simply lazy stereotypes that conceal the crucial common contemporary challenges that are shared by everyone of all ages as they shape a new long life. The danger is they seek to emphasise differences rather than commonality and so create intergenerational conflict rather than intergenerational cohesion.

Forging intergenerational empathy

Forging greater empathy between the generations is not just a way of avoiding the risk of 'generational war'. The age segregation which the three-stage life encouraged reduced our ability to benefit from one of the oldest and most rewarding forms of relationships – those that span the generations. When people of different ages purposefully interact – in colleges, the workplace, in their leisure time – they feel a sense of connection and individuality. Even if they realise that they are separated by stages of life and situated differently in the passage of time, their common purpose binds them together.

The gains to forging intergenerational empathy are substantial. The two loneliest groups of people are the young and the old.[33] It's crucial that social ingenuity is focused on creating bonds between them. That's what Georgina Binnie has achieved through her 'Writing Back' pen-pal programme at the University of Leeds, which helps forge connections between students and older people. It aims to tackle loneliness, but also to act as an exchange of knowledge and form points of contact within the community.

Efforts at trying to reignite the bonds between the generations are long-standing. As far back as 1976, a Tokyo nursery school and a care home were combined on one site. The impetus is increasing: the Singaporean government has recently committed £1.7 billion towards initiatives to improve aging, and this includes ten intergenerational housing developments. The beauty of these initiatives is that they build on the natural mutuality between the old and the young, honed by evolutionary instincts. Older people can play a crucial role in mentoring and supporting young people; in the words of child psychologist Urie Bronfenbrenner: 'every child needs at least one adult who is irrationally crazy about him or her'.[34]

In return, the young can be energising. That is how it feels for eighty-nine-year-old Londoner Fay Garcia who lives in the care home, Nightingale House. In the same location is the Apples and Honey Nightingale nursery, which Fay visits at least once a week. She considers it the highlight of her week. For the social entrepreneur Marc Freedman this is where the true fountain of youth is found. His belief is that immortality is not to be found through scientific discoveries, but rather in the lasting legacy of supporting the young. As Harvard's George Vaillant remarked, 'biology flows downhill'.[35]

COMMUNITIES

For most of us, while family, friends and work colleagues are our closest social relationships, our community forms the everyday backdrop to our life. Whether it is the neighbours in the street where you live, or the global online network you are a member of, these broader relationships are important to our well-being. But like much of our life, the combination of technology and longevity are both disrupting what previously worked success-fully, as well as offering new opportunities for social ingenuity to reinvent how communities function.

Divided communities

Our community interactions are increasingly virtual, rather than face to face. In reaching out to their community, the average Facebook user spends thirty-nine minutes each day interacting virtually, and forty-three minutes face to face.[36] Online deliveries are increasingly substituting shopping on the high street, cheap home-delivered meals replacing going out to a restaurant. Radhika works almost entirely online and rarely meets her clients. That gives her the fantastic opportunity of working remotely with people from all over the world, but it does reduce her day-to-day contact with people who live near her. We need

132

to use our social ingenuity to ensure that these new methods of connecting supplement rather than replace the deeply rewarding relationships that make us flourish as humans. This is particularly acute as communities and societies become more segregated. One aspect of this segregation is the growing proportion of people who live on their own. It is predicted that by 2030 in France, for example, this will be the case for half of all households; in Japan and England the proportion will be 40 per cent; in the US, 30 per cent; and in Korea, 24 per cent.

In part this reflects the number of older people living on their own. Today only a quarter of over eighty-five-year-olds in the US live in multigenerational households, compared to two-thirds in 1940. Often their children have moved to large cities and without these family ties older people become vulnerable to loneliness and lack of informal care. In Japan there is rising concern about *kodokushi* – lonely deaths – with older people dying alone and unnoticed, and not being found for several weeks, if not months. Technology can play a role and in Japan robots are an increasingly accepted way of assisting in the care of frail elders. These machines have their own 'personalities', can be seen almost as pets and are endowed with a sense of their own identity. When, according to Age UK, more than 40 per cent of people aged over sixty-five say their main source of companionship is their television, interacting with an intelligent robot seems a distinct improvement. For Ying, Skype has been invaluable as a way to stay in touch with her mother who lives two hundred miles away. This, combined with her mother's smart speaker Alexa reassures her that she is connected and safe. But Ying worries that the reassurance she feels from these connective technologies has meant she actually visits her mother less often.

What these new technologies are great at is matching people. That's a powerful tool with enormous potential, but inevitably it changes the nature of the collective experience. Nowhere is this more apparent than in dating. In 1980 around 35 per cent of heterosexual couples 'met through friends', or work (20 per cent) their family (18 per cent) or their college (22 per cent). In other words, they used their physical and community network.

By 2017 nearly 40 per cent of couples met online[37] and the percentage looks to be rising each year.

With this online matching comes 'assortative mating', the tendency of people to marry others who are similar to themselves. The impact of this matching is apparent in the US where in the 1960s only a quarter of male graduates married women with degrees; by 2016 that was half of male graduates married female graduates. The outcome is households where either both adults are earning high incomes, or where both are less educated and therefore likely to be earning lower incomes. The inevitable result is widening inequality.

As people are 'sorting' into similar couples, so they are also choosing to live in communities of similar people. This inevitably changes the nature of neighbourhoods and puts location and place at a premium. So higher-educated people choose to be surrounded by other higher-educated people – both recreationally and in their work. And, moreover, in order to minimise long commuting times, these highly educated and highly paid people are also choosing to live in the centre of cities. This in turn increases house prices in city centres, squeezing out low-income households and leading to greater economic segregation. In cities such as London, the median home costs around fifteen times a London salary; in Hong Kong the ratio is even higher (19.4).[38] As a result, neighbourhoods go through the process of gentrification as shops and services switch to more high-priced items – Whole Foods, Peloton bike shops, Lululemon yoga – which reinforces the presence of those with a high income and drives out others. The impact in cities such as San Francisco and San José is marked and becoming a political issue. But this isn't just a US phenomenon: in 11 out of 13 major European cities, income segregation has increased since 2001.[39]

At the same time as neighbourhoods are becoming more segregated, they are also less defined by a sense of 'shared place'. Like many freelancers, Radhika is a recent immigrant to the city and lives away from her closest family members. Without a daily workplace, she knows very few people. So for many people place could become less significant as an external reference across their lifespan. As Radhika's experience shows, after young adulthood where you live will be less a reflection of your origins and more of the choices made at different points of a multistage life.

Is all of this inevitable, or is it possible to reimagine what place and community could be? It seems unlikely that we can go back to traditional communities. But it is possible to try and build a stronger sense of community and place by actively making choices to shop locally rather than use online stores, create a book club of your neighbours rather than your old friends and colleagues, or use the local gym rather than the one by the office. However, in all these cases the forces of economics are working against communities. So the other option is to think about being a social pioneer by innovating and creating new spaces where communities come together. That's what social pioneer Jonathan Collie is doing with the establishment of 'the Common Room'.[40] For Collie this is about asking important societal questions and then creating a physical space – a 'common room' – for people of all ages and backgrounds to come together to have these conversations and take part in inclusive activities. It is just one example of the many social experiments that are underway as neighbourhoods and communities are redesigned to better suit our human needs.

Expanding community time

Traditionally the final stage of a three-stage life has been a time when people are most likely to engage with the community. In the UK, as the National Council for Voluntary Organisations (an umbrella body for the voluntary and community sector in England) has shown, volunteering starts to increase when people reach their mid-fifties and rises again as they move into their sixties. As people live longer and reach retirement age in better health and with many more years left, then the pool of potential volunteers for community-based work grows. As Marc Freedman remarks, 'old people are the only natural resource that is increasing in the world'[41].

They could be a crucial resource. Historically, volunteer organisations have played an important role in periods of transition. During the Industrial Revolution for example many communities underwent profound change as cities and factories grew. Millions of families moved to factory towns and by doing so lost the traditional forms of community support such as the rural parish or church. Over time new forms of community institutional support were created by voluntary charities and volunteers who stepped in to help and perform crucial unpaid work. Indeed, it was during this period that charities such as the YMCA (founded in London in 1844) and the Salvation Army (1865) grew in size. Much of this unpaid work was performed by women, especially those who were wealthy, educated and married. They were neither expected nor able to take paid employment – the presumption was that they would contribute through voluntary work, usually in the caring sector. A good example of this is the UK's Royal Voluntary Service (RVS, originally the Women's Voluntary Service) which had, at its peak in 1943, over a million members. While the RVS is still performing valuable charitable work, its membership has declined to only 25,000 members today.

Behind the rapid growth of such charitable activities was an awareness of social problems and a pool of people willing and able to help tackle them. Over time government policy started to address the problems and women moved into paid work, so these activities declined; the need for them was less and fewer people had the time to help. We believe the stage is set for an increase in charitable activities. Again, there are clear signs of a tough transition created by technology, and once more there is a willing pool of able people. This time, rather than under-employed women, it is an active and energetic pool of older people who want to remain engaged in purposeful activity. This is exactly the resource that Encore.org taps into with its 'Encore Fellows' program which offers people approaching retirement the opportunity to work in a sponsored role in not-for-profit organisations. Such 'Encore' careers are a natural extension of a three-stage life: they represent one way of creating a multistage life and show the broadening concept of 'work'.

This community work may not necessarily provide a pay cheque, but there are significant rewards for those who give their time and skills. Studies of mental health and life satisfaction show the overwhelmingly positive impact of volunteering.[42] People who engage with their community are more likely to live longer;[43] and the sense of purpose this brings has been shown to reduce the risk of Alzheimer's[44] and lower mortality rates.[45]

But it is not just about older volunteers. The essence of a multi-stage life is a loosening of the relationship between age and stage. Rather than focus on community work in retirement, it makes sense to distribute it across the whole of life. That's important because studies show that volunteering is rarely an activity that people begin in retirement.[46] It is the *habit* of volunteering, and the attitude of being prepared to work for no pay that is something that develops across a lifetime. In the words of Harvard Law School Professor Michael Sandel: 'Altruism, generosity, solidarity, and civic spirit are not like commodities that are depleted with use. They are more like muscles that develop and grow strong with exercise.'[47]

Community empathy: stepping behind the 'veil of ignorance'

As our societies become more segregated, there is a danger that we inevitably lack awareness, understanding and empathy of 'the other'. This diminution of empathy holds back the positive social and political processes that could fuel the social ingenuity needed to address these problems. One way of overcoming this problem is to adopt the device of Harvard political philosopher John Rawls. He suggests that when you think about the sort of society you would like to live in, you should imagine being behind a 'Veil of Ignorance'.[48] At this point, who you are is hidden from you – you are unaware of your gender, race, age, health, intelligence, skills, education or religion. Given this ignorance of your status, *what is it you would desire from your community?*

Placing yourself behind the Veil of Ignorance forces you to confront how others will deal with the shocks and transitions that are set to impact us all. In a longer life with technological transitions we will all experience more shocks and more risk. The key issue is this: what is the long-run impact of these shocks?

It is possible that across a long life you will have more time to recover from these shocks and absorb the risks. In this case where you start from will have less influence. Over a long life your path is more dependent on your own decisions.

But it is also possible that over time, bad luck accumulates. As we have shown, the longer you work, the better your finances, the more resources you have; and the more engaged you are the better your health and your motivation and the longer your healthy life expectancy. But the accumulation can also run the other way. Lower education tends to lead to lower income, leaving you with fewer resources to cope with the impact of technology on your work or ill health. This in turn creates further disadvantages making you more exposed to further ill fortune. Over a longer multistage life this would create scope for greater divergence and inequality.

However, the Veil of Ignorance isn't just a device to help form social empathy. In a longer life you have many 'possible selves'. Which ones you will occupy in the future will depend on the inter-action between your choices as well as random events outside your control. With longer horizons and greater labour market volatility, the range of possible selves you could inhabit increases and with that comes greater risk.

In the children's game of snakes and ladders the player who is able to get to the top-right corner of the board wins. Imagine that you are playing that game. You roll the dice and you land at the foot of a ladder: you can shoot upwards very quickly. But if on the roll of the dice you accidently land at the head of a snake, you move downwards, sliding rapidly to the bottom of the board. There will be events in your life which are like landing on a ladder – they will accelerate your movement upwards; there will be other events which in contrast will set you back. For instance, if you fall seriously ill then even if you are highly educated, the chances of you being able to get back to work are much reduced.[49] People who report their health is 'fair, bad or very bad' are 20 per cent less likely to be employed and even if they are employed, they earn 20 per cent less. The effect of this flows through life and into retirement through a reduced pension.

Over a longer life characterised by technological change, the game becomes longer and that means there are more ladders with the potential to move you forward, but also more snakes that push you back. And with these changes, the impact of the snakes and ladders will be ever greater.

Which brings us back to the Veil of Ignorance. In front of you over a long life there are many possible selves. Faced with such uncertainty you are less sure of your future identity; you lack insight about what your future situation will be. Under these circumstances it makes sense for you to be more interested in the support and insurance mechanisms that governments and society can offer. You might not be Estelle now, but you could be in the future – or your children could be. Our capacity to respond to the changes ahead needs the support and insurance that families and communities can offer.

YOUR RELATING

Test your plan for relationships

> *Do I have the time?* As you think about your plans for the future you will want to factor in the satisfaction and pleasure you gain from relationships – with your partner, children, family and friends. These 'pure' relationships require considerable time – time spent with others, time to create mutual trust and love, a focus on building empathy and understanding. As you look at the life path and stages you have imagined, have you allocated sufficient time for this? If there is a succession of stages that are high octane with very limited periods of downtime, then you may have to go back to your plan and consider whether you need to build in more space.
>
> *Have you discussed clearly what you want from the future?* As life extends and becomes multistage you have more options and more potential sequences. However, these new opportunities

require careful coordination with those closest to you who may be making other plans or are unaware of these new possibilities. Have you spent enough time discussing clearly and openly what you would like to do and what that entails for those around you?

Will I be able to adapt? Earlier we described how carer + career is morphing into career + career. That's a more complex relationship structure that will require all partners to be adaptive. What adaptive demands are you making on both yourself and those around you across the stages that you are proposing?

Prioritise your community

Will I spend time with my community? Take a look at the life path you are considering and evaluate it in terms of the communities you will be living in. Are these communities that will bring you joy and stretch your learning? And, in thinking about the stages of your life, will you have sufficient time to invest in your community – in supporting others and helping to build a sustainable neighbourhood? How can you build in habits that promote your engagement with those around you?

Will I be with many age groups? Your life plan will be more robust and potentially rewarding if you are able to spend time with people who are older and people who are younger than you. As you take a closer look at the stages and the activities you have in mind, are you likely to find yourself in a 'ghetto' of people the same age as you? If you are then you need to think deeply about what it would take to branch out to be with other age groups. Focus not on age but on people.

PART THREE

HUMAN SOCIETY

6

THE CORPORATE AGENDA

The practices, norms and culture established by corporations will have a major role to play in determining whether humans are able to flourish. The need for ingenuity within corporations is as great as the broader social ingenuity we have described. It is imperative that corporate practice catches up with the needs of a hundred-year life, the ebb and flow that a sixty-year career entails, and the flexibility that new technologies will demand. It will also have to catch up with the changing definition of what 'work' means.

Many people will aspire to become social pioneers and change the way they work and live. But without the framing of supportive organisational practices, these aspirations will simply turn to frustration. When working lives are relatively short, then work that is stressful might be a price worth paying for a decent pay packet. But when work is spread out across more decades, then this type of work is simply not viable. This will put an enormous premium on jobs that are re-energising and learning orientated.

Currently too many corporate policies are incompatible with human flourishing. If they continue to be inflexible, Hiroki and Madoka will be blocked from being the parents they want to be, Tom will find his upskilling efforts pointless, and Ying will be prevented from working into her seventies.

ENABLE MULTISTAGE LIVES

The three-stage life is deeply embedded in the approach of corporates to their workforce. The young are recruited as they

143

leave full-time education; 'high potentials' are promoted in their late twenties and accelerated up several more rungs of the promotion ladder; and a hard stop is established for those in their late fifties or mid-sixties. All this takes place in lockstep, ensuring that everyone goes through the same stage at the same age. By firmly equating age and stage in this way, lockstep enormously simplifies human resources policy by collapsing individual aspirations and motivations into a simple-minded dependence on chronological age.

There are real challenges here. One of the key elements of a multistage life is that it enables people to uniquely redistribute time across the course of their life and to sequence activities in a multitude of ways. But to support this, corporate policy must break the link between age and stage. This will require action on two fronts: create multiple points of entry that enable people to scale up and down their engagement with work, and refashion retirement and productivity.

Create multiple points of entry

For most companies the doors of entry swing open for people in their early twenties and then close sharply. That's why Hiroki's father is so keen for him to start work at his firm now and worries that he may lose the opportunity if he delays. He sees it as a golden opportunity for Hiroki to launch his career.

If people are to have the opportunities of a multistage life, then these entry doors must remain open for people to join at *any* point and at *any* age. When Hiroki contemplates a sixty-year career he knows he doesn't want to spend it all with one company. When many millions of young people make the same calculation, then promotion ladders will no longer be filled with ever ascending cohorts of graduate intakes. Building a talented senior cadre will therefore depend less on graduate recruitment, and more on attracting and finding people at all career stages.

The most immediate challenge with closing the doors for those beyond their mid-twenties is that it implicitly excludes anyone who spent their twenties exploring and investigating their skill set and values. Their preferred entry point could well be in their early thirties. And it's not just those in their early thirties coming back from periods of exploring and learning. People of all ages will be looking to enter the workforce in a new role. That's clear from the stories of Tom, Ying and Estelle.

There is no doubt that corporations will find recruiting at these various entry points tough. Most corporations are skilled at putting graduates through a homogenous selection process. It's a great deal more complex to judge the skills and suitability that older people have acquired in different sectors and jobs. Making the shift will require expanding from a single focus on academic credentials to a wider analysis of relevant skills, probably through exploiting data analytics and establishing new metrics. Corporations must also reconsider their view of 'gaps' in the CV, created when people choose to experiment and make transitions. From the perspective of the three-stage life, these 'gaps' are treated with suspicion. But from the perspective of a multistaged life, they should be understood and even celebrated.

Some companies are starting to create these multiple entry points. Initially focusing on returning mothers, they are now broadening their approach to the whole talent pool. Welcoming people who have taken up to two years out from work is the focus of an initiative by UK telecommunications firm O2. They run an eleven-week paid programme to reorientate people to full-time work. Barclays Bank, meanwhile, have designed an apprenticeship programme which targets all ages, including people who have been made redundant mid-career or had decided to retire early.

Three stage lives have a single entry point and are essentially linear – people advance through a set number of promotions and at some point their career reaches a plateau. By contrast, in a multistage life, careers become non-linear: there are periods of full-time work; time spent taking breaks to recharge or rebuild skills; and time out to achieve a better work–life balance. So rather than run the risk of losing valued workers who are embarking on a new stage, it makes sense for firms to offer their workforce the opportunity to ramp up and ramp down their work commitments.

145

There is much to commend this flexibility. It is a valuable recruitment and retention tool and crucially it's attractive for people like Madoka and her ever-dwindling cohort of younger workers. Sponsoring educational breaks, sabbaticals or spells of charitable work in the community is a means to achieving this.

These longer and non-linear career paths also require fresh thinking about promotion. A linear career with a hierarchical promotional structure leads to promotion blockages if people stay in a post for too long. This is particularly problematic in family firms where younger generations may have to wait a very long time before inheriting control. The British royal family is a case in point with Queen Elizabeth II at the time of writing being the oldest and longest serving English monarch at age ninety-three. Her son Prince Charles is currently seventy-one and assuming that eventually he becomes king, he will be the oldest monarch to ascend to the throne. Longevity has meant a long wait for him.

In response, companies will have to be ingenious about moving from vertical promotion to horizontal movement. They can do this by offering employees the opportunity to use their skills in a range of ways or to extend their skillsets in lateral roles, and by doing so create more flexible career ladders or career nets that will also help facilitate ramping up and ramping down. That way horizontal career shifts are seen as part of a career progression rather than a sign of a stalling career.

Refashion retirement

One of the overwhelming insights from the research on longevity is the malleability of age and the potential this has for enabling people to be economically productive into their seventies. And as we have shown, this economic activity will be crucial for the finances of both the individual and the economy. Yet many people are currently blocked from working longer by a corporate policy of retirement at the age of sixty-five or sixty or even earlier. This has to change – and fast.

There is no doubt that regulation will play a part in this change as governments begin to introduce legislation that makes age-based retirement difficult to enforce. Yet whilst some firms are offering older workers the possibility of continued employment, few have created a systematic way of supporting people to work into their seventies and eighties. Instead they offer employees a binary choice – either full-time work or full-time retirement.

This is far from what people want or need. In the words of retirement experts Joshua Gotbaum and Bruce Wolfe, 'most people hope their retirement will be like a warm bath: you work your way in slowly and gradually', whilst currently retirement is 'more like a cold shower'.[1] Companies are increasingly grasping this reality: a recent US study showed around 72 per cent of employers think their employees want to work past retirement age, and indeed almost half of them envisage some form of phased transition into retirement. The challenge is the link between the rhetoric and the reality of action – of these companies only 31 per cent actually offer part-time employment.[2]

A way to achieve this is to design optional retirement paths, including the possibility to carry on full-time as well as more flexible, phased paths to the end of work. These have to be designed and communicated ahead of time because managing expectations is crucial if people are to make plans for their future. People need to know, for example, whether they can delay retirement, work flexibly and what the consequences are in terms of time commitment and salary.

In some companies this starts early. At the Swiss–Swedish multinational ABB, as people reach the age of forty-five they are invited to attend a three-day seminar about their career development and possible milestones. This gives them an opportunity to take an early look at their options and begin to consider possible future pathways and develop new platforms. A decade later employees (with their spouses) are briefed on topics including aging at work, active life-design, finance and health in old age, and 'young and old' generational issues. By sixty those with valuable skills are given the opportunity to transfer to a consulting practice, Consenec. This is an interim management company where they are joined by executives from General Electric, Bombardier and Ansaldo Energia to work as experts in a variety of projects.

Similarly, the Japanese conglomerate Mitsubishi has created an independent company, Mitsubishi Heavy Industries, to specifically make use of the skills of workers who are past the traditional retirement age. These schemes focus on managerial positions but the gig economy offers the opportunity to refashion retirement for a wider range of workers.

A major block to extending working careers is the implicit link between age and wage. In many industries, wages rise over time with job tenure. The result is that older workers become more expensive and are therefore often the first to be laid off during economic downturns. There needs to be real social ingenuity to tackle this challenge. One way forward is to develop more flexible pay structures combined with more flexible approaches to working time. Studies show that many workers over the age of sixty would like to continue working – but often not on the same full-time basis. In a recent US study of 1,500 people over the age of fifty-five, many had a strong preference for a flexible work schedule and some were prepared to cut their wages for flexibility. In fact, almost half said they would take a 10 per cent reduction in hourly wages, and about 20 per cent would be willing to take a 20 per cent reduction in hourly wages.[3] It seems that the time has come to talk openly about age, promotion and wages.

SUPPORT HEALTHY AND HAPPY FAMILIES AND RELATIONSHIPS

A cornerstone of a fulfilling life is deep relationships within a family and within the wider community. Earlier we described the ways we imagined these could be fashioned in the future: much of this requires time, and some of it requires flexibility. The challenge is that corporate practices can put a significant brake on investing in these relationships.

How can the corporate agenda respond to longevity and technology in a way that makes it easier to combine work and family in a fulfilling way? Could ways be found that would enable men such as Hiroki to be more engaged in the joy (and frustration) of raising a family; or to ensure that Madoka does not have to choose between a career and a family? And with a growing number of older people, are there ways that work can be designed to accommodate caring for aged relatives?

We think there are – but it will take determination on the part of corporate leaders to bring about a shift in corporate practice and corporate culture.

The financial penalty of raising a family

At the heart of investing in relationships and families is the allocation of time – time to create deep partnerships and the commitments and trust they require; time to spend with young children; time to care for aging parents and time to support communities. Yet in most companies taking time out from work is not easy and usually carries a financial penalty. That's the stark experience of a group that have taken time out from work – working mothers. As we show in Figure 6.1, in both the UK and

FIGURE 6.1 Child penalties in earnings in the UK and the USA (source: "Child Penalties Across Countries: Evidence and Explanations", Kleven, Landais, Posch, Steinhauer, Zweimuller, AEA Papers and Proceedings, 109, 122-126, 2019)

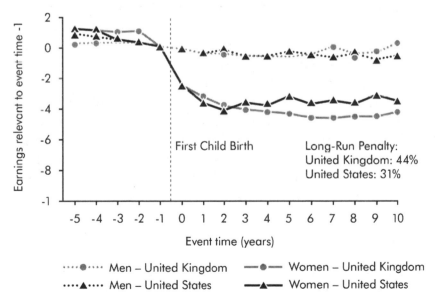

the US, women's salaries start to fall relative to men around the time a first child is born. This isn't a temporary effect either but cumulates over time, with women's salaries falling by 44 per cent and 31 per cent relative to men after ten years.[4]

This is not straightforward cause and effect; there are many reasons for this gender gap. But it seems that a key determinant is the penalty that companies impose on those who demand flexible hours and those who are not able to work longer hours. And it isn't just issues of pay that are a problem. Studies reveal the considerable frustration and in some cases depression that many mothers experience upon returning to work. Mothers have described how their skills are perceived as outdated, how the time they have taken out is viewed as a gap with no real value, and how they are penalised for being older on their return. Perhaps that is why so few actually return to their former employer – many change industry and functional roles. Often they redirect from the corporate to the social sector, and from traditionally male-dominated occupations to traditionally female-dominated ones. This in turn perpetuates the gender gap in earnings, as these sectors tend to pay less.[5]

It is clear that corporations need to focus hard on the experiences of mothers and be more supportive. There has been a plethora of initiatives, which include creating women's networks, 'on-ramp' programmes, female quotas and mentoring. Yet these, though worthy, have not had a great deal of success. Why that might be the case is revealed in the research on women and motherhood conducted by the University of Chicago Booth School's Marianne Bertrand.[6] She concludes that at the heart of inequality at work is inequality at home. Women are punished at work for supporting their family, while men are given limited support for doing so. That creates an unequal burden in furthering careers for women.

In the push for stronger and more resilient families, enabling fathers to spend more time with the family is a good place to start.

Support fathers

Studies show that positive involvement of fathers leads to better outcomes for children, for fathers themselves, and for the family as a whole.[7] Those fathers who contribute more to housework and childcare experience a lower risk of divorce and are more satisfied with their lives. Yet only a small proportion of fathers currently get the chance, or are prepared to take the chance, to nurture their children.

The take-up of paternity leave and the reasons why it differs so much from maternity leave varies across countries. This is due to government and corporate policy, along with prevailing social attitudes. In many countries governments discriminate against fathers. In the UK, a mother on an average annual income of £27,000 receives in the first year of maternity leave six weeks' state maternity pay at £466 plus 33 weeks at £141, making a total of £7,449. The total a father receives is two weeks' state paternity leave at £141, or £282. Fathers therefore receive twenty-six times less – a gender pay gap of 96 per cent. The problem is replicated on the corporate side where many companies give more generous maternity pay than is legally required and yet less than 5 per cent of companies do the same for men.[8]

One simple solution is to change government policy. A number of governments (Sweden, Norway, Quebec) are doing this through 'daddy quotas', which offer a fixed quota of parental leave to be shared between the parents but where a proportion of the months are lost if they are not taken up by the father.

As well as providing a stronger financial incentive, such policies might also shift another stubborn problem – social norms around the male role in child-rearing. Much depends on the country and the culture: in the UK, more than half of fathers say they would not take up their right to parental leave, while in Sweden, almost all fathers take paternity leave. This is because forty years ago the government introduced a gender-neutral paid-leave allowance – paying 90 per cent of wages for 180 days per child. Parents could decide between themselves how they wanted to divide this. It took many years for fathers to decide to take it up, but now the average take-up is around seven weeks.

There are also shifts occurring in corporate policy. In the USA a number of high-profile tech firms are beginning to offer paternity leave to employees. For instance, Netflix gives up to a year of paid parental leave during which parents can work, or not work as they please, while the e-commerce company Etsy gives twenty-six weeks, of which eight weeks must be taken continuously in the first six months, but employees are allowed to space out the rest over two years after the birth or adoption of a child.

Support carers

Even though on average people are aging better, it is inevitable that the shift in the age distribution of society will bring about a new family need – caring for elderly relatives. In China the one-child policy has resulted in many families with one grandchild and four grandparents, which will give a whole new meaning to 'parental leave'. This is already happening: in the UK 1 in 8 workers currently combine paid work with unpaid care responsibilities.[9] These caring demands place a burden not just on the individual but also the economy. In the UK, 1 in 4 people aged 50–64 were not in work because of their caring duties; in Spain it is 1 in 3.[10]

Looking forward, more working people will want to take time out or to work flexibly to care for elderly relatives. As with parental leave, this requires both corporate and government action. Governments can introduce carers' leave on a similar basis to parental leave. Yet it is important that the burden isn't placed disproportionately on women. Given that across the world women tend to do between two and eight times more unpaid care work than men,[11] a 'son's quota' will need to be introduced for parental care.

There is also a crucial role here for corporations. In line with its age-friendly policies, the UK energy company Centrica offers one month's paid carers' leave and flexible working hours. Their experience is that the gains in reduced absenteeism and lower staff turnover help make this an attractive proposition.

Create a culture of flexibility

Most employees experience their workplace as relatively inflexible. The result is that as events occur over the life course, so there becomes a mismatch between the hours of work you desire and the hours of work you can get. Studies have shown that when people experience this mismatch in one period of their life, they meet their preferences by changing jobs in the next period.[12]

In part corporations struggle to deliver flexibility because it conflicts with the preferred corporate structure of standardised working times and operating procedures. The consequence is that those who want to work flexibly with autonomy over their hours tend to get paid less. This creates something of a dilemma: flexible working makes it easier to raise a family or care for parents but tends to come with lower hourly pay. This inevitably puts work and relationships into direct conflict. If flexible working comes with a cost, then it doesn't solve the problem of a gender earnings gap.[13] However, there are good reasons to be optimistic that firms will tackle this dilemma going forward.

The first is simply one of supply and demand. As more people embark on a multistage life they will demand flexible work. These demands will occur at many points in their lives: older workers will want a retirement transition that gives them flexibility; parents with young children will want more time with them; those with elderly parents will want to fulfil their caring responsibilities; and as people ramp up and ramp down they too will want flexible working hours. As demand for flexible working rises, so the supply of people who are prepared to work inflexibly will dwindle, significantly reducing the talent pools that companies can recruit from. When the majority of the workforce want full-time employment, the costs of flexible hours to the firm will be substantial – but when *everyone* wants flexibility, the system becomes easier to manage.

The second reason for optimism is the four-day working week, which we believe will be a likely eventual consequence of the higher productivity created by new technologies. A four-day working week provides a great deal more scope for employees to spend time with their family and new combinations of how to work flexibly.

There is also the impact of technology. AI and robotics will change the workplace, providing new ways to work flexibly, but also offering new ways to handle data and plan complex operations. This new technology should lower the costs of firms providing more flexible employment.

The empirical research of Harvard economists Claudia Goldin and Larry Katz sheds light on how the transition to more flexible working can be achieved and how it can be prompted by technology. Flexible working is tough for corporations because in many roles it is imperative that the same person does the task over time. In other words, one employee cannot be *substituted* for another, and this reduces flexibility. However, there are industries where technology has made this substitution between workers possible. Goldin and Katz look in particular at the US pharmacy industry.[14] Over the past few decades in this sector, the hourly pay of men and women has become equal, as has the hourly pay of those who work full-time with those who work part-time. This has boosted the ability of people to work flexibly – and therefore navigate the complexity of a career + career partnership. Achieving this equality was not a result of regulation or conscious gender policies. Instead, it came from significant changes in organisational structure, technology investment and standardisation of products. From a structural perspective, as the pharmacy sector consolidated from small independent shops to larger chains it became easier for employees to switch from one store to another, and to step in and substitute for another worker in a store if they took time off. The sector also made significant technological investments in record keeping; this increased the ease of access to customer records and meant that a range of people could deal with the same customer at different times. Products were also standardised across stores, again enabling employees to substitute for one another. Clearly, organisational structure and job design can play a significant role in enhancing flexibility.

An early experiment at the UK telecoms BT more than two decades ago showed that flexibility does not have to have a trade-off with productivity: employees who worked flexibly tended to be more productive and more likely to stay with the firm.[15] Since then many initiatives such as Unilever's 'Anytime Anywhere' have supported flexible working and the current push to reduce office costs will bring more opportunities to work from home and to work flexible hours.

CHAMPION LEARNING

Lifelong learning is fundamental to a new long life, and companies play a crucial role in championing this. This is not straightforward. As more work is performed by contingent workers, and when employees are more mobile, the incentives for firms to be learning-orientated is much reduced. As Jonas Prising, CEO of the employment consultancy ManpowerGroup, remarks: 'Organisations have moved from creating talent to consuming work.'[16] With the average UK employee receiving just over sixteen hours of training a year from their employer,[17] the impetus to develop work-related skills has clearly shifted towards the individual.

Despite this backdrop, the agenda for firms must include actively championing a learning environment. An obvious motivation is to ensure the people are trained and able to use new technologies. Another incentive is that, through enabling new ways of learning, digital platforms substantially lower costs of providing training. They also create opportunities for greater customisation in ways that can be more easily measured and monitored.

Just as social media creates an array of material to choose to read and follow up on, so corporate learning platforms have the potential to give every employee options on what to read or watch. This material can be personalised and curated to build competence and enable people to work at their own pace. Effectively, it's the 'Netflixisation' of corporate training.[18] At Unilever, employees log on to the learning platform and are greeted with a curated range of options to read and watch. The platform is populated by employees' own learning insights in an effort to truly democratise the learning process. Selected employees are given up to $1,000 to attend a conference or take a course. They then produce their own learning materials which they put onto the learning platform so others can access. How are the employees selected? Based on how often their own recommendations on what to read and watch on the platform are followed by others. As Tim Munden, global chief learning officer for Unilever, says, the idea is that 'leading edge people know best what they and others need to learn'.[19]

Across the world companies are making similar investments in learning platforms. At the Indian IT company Tata Consultancy Services, the internal platform 'Knome' enables more than 420,000 employees to track the development of their skills and build their reputation by acquiring virtual 'badges' for the skills they have developed.

While low-cost platforms are a route to triggering curiosity, some companies are making more significant financial investments in helping people learn from across their working life. That is the focus for United Technologies (UTC), the corporation which includes the development of aircraft engines for Pratt & Whitney. Investing in employee skills has been a priority since 1996, when the company decided to pay tuition fees of up to $12,000 for any employee who wanted to take a part-time degree. It could be argued that UTC is simply educating employees for rivals. But Gail Jackson, the vice president of human resources, sees it as an investment: 'We want people who are intellectually curious. It is better to train and have them leave, than not to train and have them stay.'[20]

Other investors in learning are in sectors that are experiencing significant disruption. So, rather than recruit a new cohort of workers, they are investing in retraining their current workforce. At AT&T, the US telecoms and media firm, which has over 300,000 employees, over the last decade the core business strategy has moved from traditional telecoms to big data and cloud computing. Re-orienting the business strategy has gone hand in hand with upskilling and reskilling the workforce. The learning process began with each employee creating a career profile and recording their skills and training. Armed with this they were able to access the 'career intelligence' database which showed the jobs available within the company and the reskilling needed to perform them. They could then use an array of nanodegrees developed with the Massive Open Online Courses (MOOC) provider Udacity and a number of universities. Whilst much of the focus is on self-directed learning, the company provides significant financial support (totalling $30 million in 2015).

Corporate commitment to lifelong learning cannot only be aimed at skilled workers. Starbucks pays the tuition fee for their staff to take online degrees with Arizona State University in a scheme only for those without an undergraduate degree. With 18,000 staff enrolled and 2,400 graduated, the aim is to reduce financial stress by increasing promotability as well as acting as a retention tool.

DITCH AGEISM

The AARP report that two-thirds of workers aged 45–74 say they have experienced ageism. Ageism is especially acute in Silicon Valley, where over the last decade the largest firms have faced more age bias cases than race or gender cases.[21] It seems that the real problem society faces is not a shortage of people capable of working – but a shortage of companies willing to give older workers a job.

At the heart of this (facial) discrimination are simple stereotypes. In many corporate boards and human resource functions there is a widespread assumption that older people are less productive and less likely to learn. No better example can be given than the succinct words of a twenty-three-year-old Mark Zuckerberg, CEO of Facebook, when he said – 'young people are just smarter'. Imagine saying the same about any other demographic group. This reveals just how acceptable it remains to make ageist remarks.

But the outlook for older workers is not entirely bleak. Since 1998 90 per cent of the rise in employment in the US is accounted for by workers aged fifty-five and over. If these increases can be achieved in the presence of ageist policies, then tackling ageism will create even more scope for further gains.

Underpinning this corporate ageism and the belief that older workers are less productive are three outdated assumptions: that older workers have less time ahead of them and so are less interested in reskilling; are less educated and therefore less productive; and are physically constrained and unable to work.

With regard to older workers having less time ahead of them, as we have already noted, a seventy-seven-year-old today has the same remaining lifespan as a sixty-eight-year-old had in 1972. Similarly, we know that people will need to work for longer as their careers lengthen. All of this will motivate older workers to continue to work and learn new skills.

The stereotype that older people are less educated is increasingly out of date. Certainly in the US in the 1950s, for example, the average seventy-year-old represented a cohort in which just half had attended school between the ages of 5–19. Mark Zuckerberg could plausibly argue that in the 1950s young people were just smarter. And by the 1980s, the overwhelming majority of sixty-five-year-olds still weren't college graduates: this was a cohort educated in the 1940s when only 7 per cent of people aged 20–24 were enrolled in college. But that's changed and currently people in their sixties are much more likely to have some form of a graduate degree. These age stereotypes therefore are not a reflection of age itself, but rather of educational policies of past ages.

The final assumption is that older people cannot work. That might have been true in the early 1960s when half of jobs in the US private sector needed at the very least moderately intense physical work.[22] But today it is less than 20 per cent and declining fast. In other words, not only are older people on average physically healthier, but the role of physical work is declining. This effect should get even stronger in the years ahead as robotics support the performance of physical labour, and AI serves as a kind of cognitive prosthetic.

Maintaining productivity in older workers

Of course, in some physical jobs, such as construction, labouring and sport, there is a decline in productivity with age. It may happen later than previously and at a slower pace, but as people age they will inevitably be less productive. At the age of thirty-eight, Roger Federer is still ranked as the third best male tennis player in the world, but eventually even his lengthy career will come to an end. These are not jobs that can support working into old age, even allowing for a greater role for robotics.

However, there is surprisingly little robust evidence showing the relationship between age and productivity and certainly no simple correlation. The malleability of age shows the variance in the way that people will age and different sectors place different demands on employees. It also turns out that there are many other variables, such as education, that exert a much bigger influence on productivity than age alone. That means that thinking about the type of jobs people do and how to structure the work environment can help keep people productive for longer.

For instance, when it comes to cognitive jobs, the crystalline intelligence of older workers can be a real advantage. This was clear from a study of productivity at a BMW manufacturing plant in Germany which found that older workers were more productive than younger ones. They discovered that whilst older workers were slightly more likely to make mistakes, younger workers were more likely to make big mistakes.[23] It seemed that the experience and crystallised intelligence of older workers helped them to be more aware of how to deal with problems and how to contain them. Similar results have come from team performance, with evidence from some companies showing that having older team members improves team performance. There is also evidence that 'grit' – as in a form of perseverance – also increases with age.[24]

A final challenge to supporting longer careers is that because most people have traditionally stopped work in their fifties, firms have not designed work with older people in mind. One option is simply to acknowledge that age stereotypes are outdated and encourage older people to work in the same manner they did previously. This doesn't require any redesign of work, and just leverages the fact people are aging better.

Another option is to purposely redesign work to support older workers. One way of doing this is to take advantage of the fact that peak circadian rhythms shift with age – from evenings (for the young) to mornings (for the older). In the summer of 2019 the McDonald's restaurant chain partnered with the AARP to fill 250,000 jobs with older workers. In a tight labour market, the company was particularly struggling to find workers motivated to do the breakfast shift. Targeting older workers (and their morning circadian rhythm) seemed a natural step. Melissa Kersey, McDonald's US chief people officer, says: 'We're looking to position McDonald's as a place where people at every stage of working life can see themselves grow and thrive while bringing stability and a different perspective that everyone can learn from.'[25]

There are also ways to alleviate the impact of any physical decline on productivity. In the same BMW assembly plant mentioned earlier, the firm provides stools for older workers and operates the assembly line at a slightly slower pace.

There is also the option of crafting new roles or creating what hotelier and author Chip Conley calls the role of the 'Modern Elder'. Building from his own experience as a member of the senior team at Airbnb, Conley describes the impact he had in his mid-fifties in a company with an average age of twenty-six. He was committed to bring his experience, leverage the ability of the whole team, and help them avoid pitfalls. These are crucial roles in the emerging typology of work – perhaps the 'Modern Elder' will be one of those new job categories.

This idea that older workers bring different skills to the workplace was explored by London Business School's Julian Birkinshaw and co-authors.[26] They surveyed more than ten thousand managers aged 21–70 across more than twenty countries about their management style. They discovered that the older the manager, the less they valued first impressions and the more emphasis they placed on being aware of how their actions affected others. Similarly, when implementing corporate strategy, they put less emphasis on business models, and more on anticipating the emotional reactions of others. In general, they discovered that older managers were more oriented toward collaboration – building rapport, building coalitions of support, and anticipating problems and concerns.

What is striking is how older workers tend to be better equipped with the very human skills that are forecast to dominate the labour market in the wake of impending technological change. Finding ways to redefine roles so as to give older workers a better chance of exploiting their comparative advantage will be important for longer working careers, but also for aiding corporate performance.

WHY SHOULD FIRMS BOTHER?

The corporate agenda we have laid out will inevitably involve many reforms that will be complicated, expensive and distracting. We have justified this primarily on the basis of individual needs for a multistage life and a longer working career. The obvious question is: Why should firms bother?

In truth, many firms won't. While they may choose to adopt some of the measures, overall the whole range will be viewed as too costly and difficult to implement. In these cases, government legislation and regulation will need to force firms to adopt these measures. However, there are also many firms for whom introducing these measures will be crucial for ensuring they remain competitive.

The importance of an agile workforce

A constant theme of business thinking in recent years has been the need to develop a fast and agile corporate environment.[27] There is a clear understanding that technological change will require more flexible ways of working and demand rapid responses in how employees perform their roles. To be fast and agile people need to feel motivated and engaged. If the culture or practices of the corporation leave them exhausted, or worried about their family, or angry about not taking time out, or frustrated about the lack of learning support they are getting, or anxious about whether they can upskill fast enough, then inevitably their performance will rapidly deteriorate. Many of the measures we have described will underpin an overall 'agility' strategy and maximise the gains from technology.

The benefits of a new corporate 'pension'

In the past one of the great attractions of joining and staying with a firm was the corporate pension. This was often in the form of a defined benefit, in the sense that the final pension was a percentage of final salary. These pensions were introduced not primarily out of social concern for the workforce, but rather as a significant aid to recruitment and retention. That's because the costs of hiring workers are substantial and employee turnover is expensive. The pension made it easier to hire someone at a lower salary *now* in return for a pension in the *future*. It also strengthened retention as the pension accrued faster if the employee stayed with the firm. This traditional financial pension is becoming increasingly expensive as people are living and retiring for longer and, as a consequence, firms have moved away from them.

What could come in its place? The essence of a multistage life is that employees are interested not only in their future finances but also in developing their other less tangible assets. These assets can include their health, their skills and their capacity to navigate transitions. So our suggestion is that corporations widen the concept of a pension to go beyond simply accruing future financial assets to also supporting and investment in intangible assets, as well as offering career paths that can help navigating a multistage life. Offering mid-career breaks, the opportunities to take paid external training courses, or having options to ramp up or ramp down work commitments could all form part of this broader concept of a corporate pension.

Matching consumers and employees

It is not just employees who face ageism, it's also consumers. This is clear from the market segmentation that many firms use to organise their market data. Typically, this is in five-year intervals (i.e. 21–25; 26–30). Yet in considering people over the age of sixty-five, marketers only have one category.

The result is a real lack of insight into the fastest growing 'emerging market' – the so-called 'silver economy'. The AARP calculates that in the US the spending power of those aged over fifty is currently $7.6 trillion – making it the third largest economy in the world. These older consumers will transform the economy in profound ways, particularly in industries such as pharmaceuticals and health care, the financial sector and consumer products (notably senior living, care, age-related real estate, anti-aging products and travel and leisure).[28] But exploiting this may not be so easy for firms. Clive, like many of his age, doesn't respond well to products that are explicitly marketed for older people. He's not interested in being stereotyped or bunched into a single 'over 65' category; he is drawn instead to attributes such as ease of use, health and hygiene.

The negative age stereotypes that corporations have within the firms are also mirrored in the stereotypes that they have about older consumers. As MIT's Joseph Coughlin notes, firms too often forget the 'F factor' – fun. They may be surprised, for example, that a quarter of dating site Match.com members are aged between 53–72. Moreover, they represent the fastest growing market segment.

Whilst too many firms seem poorly set up to address the needs of this marketplace, there are those who are exercising ingenuity. The global network organisation, Aging 2.0, founded by Stephen Johnston and Katy Fike to 'accelerate innovation to address the biggest challenges and opportunities in aging', has already created a community of over 40,000 innovators from across more than twenty countries who are collaborating on creating products related to engagement and purpose, through to end of life. If firms can avoid ageism in their recruitment and retention policies, they are more likely to have a workforce who understand the needs of older consumers.

The scarcity of workers

Waves of people over the age of fifty-five are leaving the workforce and this will create serious shortages of skilled labour. In Germany, for example, there are around 4 million people aged 15–19 who will be entering the labour force in the next decade.

By contrast, there are more than 6 million people in Germany between the ages of 55–59, many of whom are probably following the three-stage life and expecting to retire any time soon.

In other words, firms are seeing a larger generational cohort exit the labour force than the one that is joining. They are faced with millions of people with experience and crystallised knowledge leaving work, and the situation will only become worse if, as seems likely, immigration flows around the world start to decline. It is crucial that firms broaden their assumptions about who can work if they are to avoid rising wages and a loss of skills. Since 2012 in Japan, the working age population has fallen by more than 5 million, but at the same time employment has risen by nearly 4.5 million. That is due to increased employment of women and workers aged over sixty-five. Given these trends, firms who succeed at recruiting or retaining workers who traditionally were not a priority, will have a key competitive advantage in an aging society.

Technology is transforming the way firms operate and is becoming a key force in the redesign of work. Longevity is transforming people's view of the relationship between work and time and indeed what counts as work. Already these forces are bringing about deep-seated changes in corporate policies. The nexus between longevity and the technological will become ever more powerful: so it is crucial, therefore, that firms adapt now – not just to enable human flourishing, but also to ensure their own success.

7

The Education Agenda

Education is ultimately about preparing people for life and increasingly that has meant a focus on preparing people for work. That is because in the labour market, education is in a race with technology. If your education can keep ahead, then your job and income prospects remain healthy.[1]

During the late nineteenth and early twentieth century this race between education and technology was the impetus behind governments making primary and secondary schooling compulsory. Technological advances also shaped how people learnt. In the early twentieth century the managerial principles of 'Taylorism' took hold in the factory, creating a focus on the standardisation of processes, the efficiency of work and the mass production of goods. The same principles underpinned the development of educational institutions and curriculums. Schools unified their teaching practices, specialised curriculums, and measured success by student grades. This standardisation helped manage the increasing volume of students and, more importantly, equipped them for the needs of the modern workplace – getting students used to continuous assessment, sitting down for long periods of set hours and taking instruction from a leadership figure.

In the absence of change, this form of education system will simply be preparing people for a life that no longer exists and for jobs that are no longer available. Obvious changes need to occur. People will need *more* education as they live and work for longer. This extra education will need to be *spread out* over time rather than be front-loaded at the beginning of life. And if learning is no longer front-loaded then what needs to be learnt *at the beginning* must focus less on specific skills and knowledge and more on learning how to build the foundations for a lifetime of learning. As the social philosopher Eric Hoffer remarked: 'In times of drastic change it is the learners who inherit the future. The learned usually find themselves equipped to live in a world that no longer exists.'[2]

Focus on human skills

The foundation of much current education assumes a *scarcity* of knowledge. The role of the teacher is to impart facts and test students on their retention of them. However, recall that in 2018 Internet traffic was estimated to be 1.8 zettabytes[3] – or more than all the words humans have written in their entire history. The world has transformed from having a scarcity to an abundance of knowledge.

This transformation requires a major change in how and what we learn. A shift in the education system from the idea of 'students' who acquire knowledge, to the notion of 'learners' who acquire skills and the ability to apply them. As Satya Nadella, the CEO of Microsoft, succinctly remarked: 'The "learn it all" will always trump the "know it all" in the long run.'[4] The implication is that from an early stage, teaching has to focus on discovering where knowledge lies, dealing with ambiguity and uncertainty, and assessing and evaluating insights to solve a particular problem. These are the very human skills which Hans Moravec describes in his 'landscape of human competencies' as being least likely to be performed by a machine. Superimposing onto this the implications of longer working lives serves only to emphasise the crucial role of learning *how* to learn and discover (as well as how to 'unlearn').

It isn't just the human skills of critical thinking, hypothesis framing and synthesis that will be in demand from the education system. Given the rising tide of Moravec's landscape, the salary premium attached to communicating, teamwork and interpersonal skills will also inevitably increase. Angela Ahrendts, former vice president of retail at Apple Inc., understands the importance of this when she says: 'the more technologically advanced our society becomes, the more we need to go back to the basic fundamentals of human connection'.[5]

Beyond STEM

In a sense this emphasis on human skills runs counter to the widespread advice to focus on STEM (Science, Technology, Engineering and Math). There is no doubt that the future ingenuity of AI and robotics will create ever more STEM jobs. In the UK the prediction is that by 2022 a further 518,000 workers will be needed in the top three digital occupational roles alone.[6] That's three times the number of the UK's computer science graduates of the last ten years. This suggests a STEM education should be a distinct advantage in a challenging jobs market. But given that graduate unemployment rates in computer science are relatively high compared to other areas, a focus on digital skills alone may be limiting.

If digital skills are necessary but not sufficient, then what other skills make the difference? When a team at Google analysed performance data on more than 10,000 top managers (most of whom would have had strong STEM skills), their interest was in which human qualities drove internal advancement.[7] They discovered that those who made the greatest contributions possessed the very human skills of being a good coach, empowering others, being interested in the well-being of the team, being a good communicator and listener, and having a clear vision and strategy.

So whilst the cost of not having digital skills and being computer literate will increase, this doesn't mean a sole focus on these skills is an appropriate response. Instead it's the combinations that will be really valuable. This explains why there is a growing interest, both in schools and universities, in STEAM courses – where the science is strengthened by the inclusion of arts.

The danger of focusing solely on STEM is that it can overemphasise the passive absorption of technical cognitive knowledge. What will be most important are the more complex skills of experimentation and risk-taking, experiential learning and collaboration and on creative problem-solving. In other words, the very hallmarks of the scientific method: of being curious, framing a hypothesis, testing, analysing and reflecting and advancing forward with better understanding.

THE CRUCIAL RISE OF ADULT EDUCATION

David Blake and Kelly Palmer of Degreed, an educational technology company providing lifelong learning platforms for corporates, make an interesting point. If you ask someone how healthy they are now and they told you they ran a marathon twenty years ago, you would find their answer strange and uninformative. Yet when we ask about a person's education, we accept as relevant and informative the response that they studied economics twenty years ago.[8]

We think of our health as something we need to monitor and invest in at every stage of life. The same will now hold true for our education, as the race between technology and education enters a new phase. If the Industrial Revolution saw rapid growth in primary and secondary education, the decades ahead will see the most rapid growth in adult education.

The concept of 'adult education' is hardly new, and is already addressed by corporate training, evening courses, returning to college, or distance learning. However, moving forward, adult education will have to become both a great deal more extensive and take a more central role in educational institutions. It must become more focused on the needs of adults, show greater flexibility and be less age agnostic as well as diversify away from degrees.

Adult focused

A cornerstone of human flourishing is the capacity to explore, to learn and to transform and that means learning as an adult. That will require changes in *how*, *who* and *what* is taught, if the needs of adults are to be met.

The 'how', according to Malcolm Knowles, an expert in the method and practice of adult learning – or 'andragogy' – has a number of attributes: it must involve the student in planning and evaluating their learning; it must be experiential so students can learn from doing; it must be problem-focused so it connects to real-life experiences; and it must be directly applicable to the learner's job and/or to their personal life.

Of course, these attributes are important for how teaching must evolve for all ages. However, a distinctive feature of adult education is that invariably people are learning at the same time as wrestling with a number of other claims on their time – work, raising a family or caring for elderly relatives. And they could be experiencing heightened anxiety as they worry about learning and getting a new job or just dealing with the social pioneering attitude of going back to school in later life. All of this makes adult education different, and that has implications for who will provide this education.

If our existing institutions are to meet the growing demand for adult education they will need to change and alter both their offerings and their delivery. In particular they will need to be more focused on employment-related issues and the specific needs and circumstances of the individual. Ying looks back and wishes she had taken a part-time course to upskill, perhaps learning some of the digital accounting skills that would have helped her keep her job. What she needs is a pedagogy that embraces Knowles's characteristics: fact-based learning, gaining competence through application, and building on existing knowledge.

However, adult learning isn't just about learning job-related skills, it is also about supporting people through transitions. That's certainly crucial for Estelle who wants to reskill and qualify as a beautician. That would be part of a major transition and so she needs people who can support her through this shifting identity. For her, an adult education learning community would really help, creating an opportunity for her to share with others who are facing similar challenges and struggles.

This touches on another distinctive feature of how adult education will evolve. At the core of a multistage life is self-awareness linked to periodical reassessment of values, purpose and the motivating forces that drive actions. In childhood and young adulthood, school and college were formative experiences, places where lifelong friendships were forged and character and values were shaped. As life extends, there needs to be an equivalent for lifelong learners who would really benefit from another round of such formative experiences. If education helps give people momentum and direction in their early twenties, why can't it do the same for those in their forties, fifties or sixties? Universities already provide such communities for those who are learning to live independently as adults and transitioning from the family home to work. Similar communities need to be built to support the adult transitions that a multistage life creates.

Flexible and navigable

The schemas and pathways we showed earlier demonstrate that at any point in time people are faced with important choices to be made and possible future selves to be explored. Learners will benefit greatly from being able to navigate and create connections between the different paths they choose. Educational institutions can support this by explicitly providing linkages between what people learn early on, and what they can build upon later. In a three-stage life educational institutions provided a platform upon which careers were built. In a multistage life with many different paths and possible selves, education needs to be much more flexible and adaptive to an individual's unique career path.

This has important implications for the focus of educational institutions. In the US the senior leadership team at Georgia Institute of Technology commissioned a report on the future of education entitled 'Creating the Next'.[9] One of the commission's predictions was that Georgia Tech should prepare for lifelong learners forming the majority of their students rather than the current 18–24-year-old cohort. This preparation is already apparent in the current 33,000 'non-traditional' learners who are enrolled there in a variety of lifelong learning courses. This focus on lifelong learners has also been crucial to the University of California Irvine's Division of Career Pathways, which was tasked with providing career support for both students and alumni. They are adamant that if the university is to deliver on its promise of lifelong learning, then it has to be prepared and able to deliver the same service to all ages throughout their career. An inevitable consequence of this shift towards lifelong learning is the blurring of the distinction between students and alumni.

What these educational early adopters are demonstrating is a fundamental shift in focus from the provision of degree-based products, to the development of learning services which include coaching, counselling and supporting the human skills that employers demand. They must also provide more opportunity for learners to decide for themselves how to sequence their learning and education. Some people will choose to initially engage in two rather than four years of college, with the aim of returning later for an additional two years. And just as work will need multiple entry points, so educational institutions will need to create multiple entry and exit points. Inevitably this flexibility will have profound implications on curriculum design, particularly in a greater modularity in course design and enhanced micro-credentialing at course rather than degree level. These shorter courses have the advantage of exercising a student's learning muscle, ensuring their skills are updated in the face of technological change whilst being easier to combine with work and family commitments.

As a result of these developments we can imagine that tertiary education will become more varied and flexible in the years ahead. It is clear that the current, standardised offerings of three- or four-year programmes cannot match the flexibility that people will aspire to. As with the corporate agenda, expect a clash between the standardised and structured institutional processes that support a three-stage life and the more flexible and customised processes demanded of a multistage life.

Age agnostic

This three-stage model of life has resulted in educational institutions being extremely age-segregated. Looking forward, the role of lifelong learning will not simply be the provision of education to a broader range of age groups, but also *blending* these age groups together.

There is plenty of evidence that intergenerational mixing is good for all. Indeed, in those training courses which develop job-related skills and knowledge, this is a natural place for the ages to mix. People have a shared common goal of achieving employment, and the work experience of older people provides valuable spill-over benefits for younger students.

Such programmes are already beginning to emerge. In 2015, Philip Pizzo, the former dean of the Stanford School of Medicine, launched the Stanford Distinguished Careers Institute (DCI). This is a one-year programme which 'offers people in midlife with major career accomplishments the opportunity to renew their purpose, develop new communities and recalibrate wellness, and to transform themselves for new roles with social impact'.[10] Importantly, while participants follow their own specific programme they also share undergraduate courses with younger students. For Pizzo, this intergenerational mixing is not simply a by-product of the programme; it's a key output. He is adamant it adds to the learning experience and, more importantly, helps the DCI fellows with their own rejuvenation and repurposing. And, given their extensive career experience, it also helps with mentoring undergraduates. As adult learning expands in this way, it provides a great opportunity to break down age silos and help each age group support one another.

Less reliant on degrees

Traditionally, the decision to enrol for a university degree was a smart move. Take, for example, the experience in the US where between 1982–2001, average wages earned by American workers with a bachelor's degree rose by 30 per cent. During the same period, those of high-school graduates did not budge. In general, analysis of unemployment rates has shown that unemployment rates decline when education achievements go up. However, the average premium for a college degree has been falling in recent decades.[11] College-educated workers are also increasingly taking on jobs for which they are overqualified as the number of graduating students has significantly outstripped the creation and availability of high-skilled jobs. By 2016 in the UK, more than half of graduates were working in what have been described as non-graduate roles.[12] As a consequence of these developments, the value of a degree has become more dependent on the subject studied, the skills learnt and the reputation of the degree-awarding institution.

At the same time, the cost of degrees has become ever more expensive. Take the US, where between 1988–2018 the cost of four-year degrees at public institutions rose by over 200 per cent above inflation. That had a profound knock-on effect on student debt which in the US now stands at over $1.5 trillion. That's larger than either credit card debt or auto loans. In the UK, where college education was until 1998 free, tuition fees now cost up to £9,250 per annum, total student debt is more than £100 billion and rising fast. Inevitably this is leading to a growing percentage of student loan defaults. In the US around 11 per cent of student loans are in default, whilst in the UK it is predicted that only around 17 per cent of students will repay their educational debt in full. That will leave the majority of people paying off their loans into their forties and fifties.[13]

The impact of these trends is that as the education market grows, disproportionately more of this growth will occur in the non-degree sector. With the average US student graduating with $37,000 debt and the average UK student £50,000, unless life-long learning is factored into the initial cost of a degree, people will inevitably resort to shorter, less expensive courses in later life. Further, if the value of a degree early on becomes more uncertain, then it may make sense to earn smaller modular credentials that can then be built on and augmented later in life.

Technological ingenuity is spurring the creation of these courses. Take for example the nanodegrees offered by the edu-tech company Udacity. Students engage between ten and twenty hours a week over a six- to twelve-month period to complete and learn skills aimed at entry-level technology jobs. These shorter courses are popular with adult learners precisely because they support reskilling and open up future options.

The good news for the education system is that the continued growth it has benefited from over the last hundred years looks set to continue. However, the bad news is that going forward, this will be focused on areas which are currently poorly served – adult education, skills and employment-based learning, and shorter, modular and cumulative programmes.[14] It also has to show real ingenuity in developing trust, building credentials, establishing inclusiveness and accelerating the role of technology.

Caveat emptor

The aim of an education is fundamentally: learn what you don't know. That creates a problem; if you don't yet know something, it's hard to evaluate whether what is on offer is any good. For instance, when Tom googles 'coding courses' he is presented with a plethora of 'schools' that offer online and in-person courses at a range of prices. How does Tom choose from these?

Tom is facing the classic problem of *asymmetric information* – he does not have sufficient insight to make a good choice. Under these circumstances, many people simply choose to register for a course with a particular provider they already know, or who others know. They don't feel they have the 'know-how' to curate their own educational experiences.

This is an issue that has to come high on the agenda for the education sector. It is clear that lifelong learning will increasingly involve non-degree courses where standards and validation are more variable. Moreover, there will be a significant number of new educational institutions formed, some for-profit, and this will inevitably lead to greater uncertainty in evaluating courses and providers. The danger is that people waste their money on educational products that make overstated claims. Indeed the more people attempt to curate their own self-directed study, the more this will become a problem. The agenda is clear: just as financial services are subject to considerable regulatory scrutiny, so too there must be increased regulation to address claims about the returns on investing in education. To do this the industry must form its own alliances and standards to help reassure potential learners of the credibility of what is on offer. Reliable data on employment rates achieved by students upon course completion will be one key measure. In the absence of transparent, credible and uniform measures of how successful courses are, the educational sector runs the same mis-selling risks that are common in the financial sector.

Build stackable and portable credentials

What is needed to overcome this asymmetric information problem is the creation of reliable credentials that can be readily recognised by both employers and learners. When lifelong learning is made up of smaller and more frequent portions of time in education, then the skill development needs to be cumulative in ways that can be measured ('stackable') and where its value is recognised across many firms and sectors ('portable').

The issue of credentialing is crucial to the lifelong learning agenda. Currently educational credentials are based on certificates such as degrees. A degree is literally a piece of paper, the attainment of which, potentially, can bring significant financial benefit. But is the certificate proof that an individual has accumulated useful skills? If it were, then surely employers would be far more interested in the details of your transcript that records scores on each course taken.

An alternative explanation is the *signalling theory* of education, for which Michael Spence received a Nobel Prize in Economics. His argument was that most employers want to hire people of high ability, but they need a way of determining who these people are. It could be that education is costly to achieve (in terms of fees and lost income) and provides no useful skills. However, if the course can only be passed by high-ability individuals, then it acts as a signal for employers. Under this assumption, education doesn't itself actually boost productivity, and so those with lower abilities will not take the course as they will learn nothing and are

175

less likely to pass. The educational qualification therefore acts to screen out less able people.

As Kelly Palmer and David Blake ask in their book on the 'expertise economy': 'If you had to choose between having an education at Harvard but no certificate of qualification or being given a Harvard degree certificate without attendance which would you prefer?'[15] The answer to that question says a lot about your own views on whether education enhances productivity or just acts as a signal.

Ultimately what employers really want is information about a person's skills and a way to select the best candidates. Degree certificates, testimonials and interview performance are the imperfect way this is currently achieved. The agenda is clear: a better way of providing credentials for everything that an individual has learnt, whether formally at an institution or on the job, and a method of easily mapping institutional qualifications into practical measurements are required.

Big data and AI could play a key role here by providing a verifiable way of measuring learning and expertise. The aspiration is that, just as the machine learning behind the Netflix platform is able to discern and predict an individual's viewing patterns, so the same can be done with skills. By monitoring learning activities (experiences, reading, job experiences) a multi-dimensional profile of skills could be formed. This is then used to identify the gap between current knowledge and future needs, with algorithms suggesting courses to help fill the gap and test progress. Looking forward, it seems to us that the greatest educational gift of AI might not be as a platform for learning but in providing ways to measure, monitor and credentialise what an individual knows from their actions and outputs.

A particular challenge here will be around the areas of 'soft skills' – those important human skills that will be in demand given shifts in technology. Between 1980–2012 jobs requiring high levels of social interaction grew by nearly 12 per cent as a share of the US labour force, whilst maths-intensive jobs actually fell over the same period.[16] Many of the short courses that have been successfully developed online are focused on technological

176

skills such as coding. The issue will be how to scale up in an employment-friendly way courses based around core human skills such as empathy, judgement and collaboration.[17] We expect this to change as new developments, particularly using virtual reality technologies, are able to simulate and support face-to-face interactions.[18]

The big questions are recognition and development. Looking forward, how long will it take employers to recognise these new credentials, and how will they be developed by academic institutions, private sector providers, employers and regulators? At the heart of this will be the need for a systematic move by either regulators or academic institutions towards a voluntary standard. A failure to achieve this will prevent adult education being the crucial support for our longer lives.

Create an inclusive learning system

The opportunity of lifelong learning must be available to everyone – be they unemployed, in jobs with little corporate support, or with insufficient income to finance themselves. In part this is an argument for social justice – everyone should have the right to flourish in an evolving world. Moreover, the mass provision of adult education is central to ensuring the economy benefits and reaps the productivity gains available from technology and longevity. A sixty-year career consisting of forty years of productive work and twenty years of unemployment or low-paid jobs monitoring smart machines, will be a lost economic opportunity and a social problem.

Creating an inclusive learning system must be high on governments' agendas and without this, adult education is likely to remain the preserve of the wealthy. Already adult education is most often used by those with a strong educational background.[19] That makes it even more important that government works to widen access, particularly to those with low skills who are more vulnerable to the impact of technology. Some governments are already taking steps. In Singapore since January 2016, every citizen over the age of twenty-five has been encouraged to upskill and retrain with the support of an initial SkillsFuture credit of S$500 ($345), with the possibility of further periodic top-ups. Citizens can spend this on training provided by any of 500 approved providers, including universities and Massive Open Online Courses (MOOCs). In 2016 the programme had a budget of S$600 million a year, planned to rise to S$1 billion by 2019.

Another possibility is the state providing, over a person's lifetime, a total of twelve months of paid income support, conditional upon taking some form of employment-related accredited training. Such a scheme would support Estelle through the beautician's course she wants to take. Governments can also regulate to require firms to provide employees, after a fixed period of employment, the statutory right to take leave for a fixed period of study and for their job to be kept open for them, just as is currently the case with maternity leave. Some countries, such as the United States and Singapore, are already offering lifetime learning tax credits. But there is no doubt that the scale and generosity of these will need to increase.

Another popular suggestion is to encourage the creation of 'Individualised Learning Accounts'. These allow, up to a certain limit, tax relief to be claimed on money put into the account for the purposes of future educational needs, similar to tax incentives for pensions. Governments could also require firms to pay into an individual's learning account when they get hired, or to offer more generous tax incentives to redundancy payments that were put into such an account.

Some education providers are also brokering 'income share agreements' with learners. These operate differently from a standard student loan and are more like a co-investment by the provider in a student. Under these schemes the course fees are financed and no repayments are made until the student's salary goes above a certain level. At this point a fixed percentage is taken for a specified period of time. Given the rising importance of education in a multistage life, expect social ingenuity to step in to create ever more innovative products to support the finances of lifelong learning.

However, providing the means to finance educational courses won't make them inclusive if their cost is prohibitive. The Stanford Distinguished Careers initiative described earlier costs around $70,000 in tuition alone – clearly out of the reach of the vast majority of people. Could something similar but less expensive be developed for everyone? Our hope is that it will. In this optimism we rely on 'Varian's Rule'[20] – that 'a simple way to forecast the future is to look at what wealthy people have today – middle-income people will have something equivalent in ten years, and poor people will have it in an additional decade'. Much social ingenuity will need to be focused on developing low-cost large-scale programmes that support people at key moments of their life to review their life plan and goals.

There is already evidence of ingenious experiments in this direction. Take the UK, for example, where the 2017 government-sponsored 'Cridland Review of the State Pension Age' recommended establishing a 'midlife MOT',[21] envisioned as a holistic lifestyle review that examines skills, finances, health and relationships and then assesses future paths and aims. A number of organisations are experimenting with the implications: the insurance companies Aviva and Legal & General, the government agency the Pensions Advisory Service, and the human capital consultancy Mercer, are all running pilot schemes. In the education sector, Dublin City University, describing itself as an 'Age-Friendly University (AFU)', runs an 'Advanced Transitions Programme' aimed at providing 'the tools, resources, learning and time for reflection necessary to make this next life phase your best yet' and is part of a global network of AFUs.

However, even as the awareness of the importance of lifelong learning is rising, in many countries the adult education sector is struggling, especially around part-time, non-degree learning. In the UK, university undergraduate programmes have expanded dramatically, but from 2004–16 the number of adult learners has almost halved. Part-time study has been hit particularly hard. Reversing this trend must be high on the agenda. As a 2017 McKinsey Global Institute report starkly notes: 'this may require an initiative on the scale of the Marshall Plan, involving sustained investment, new training models, programmes to ease worker transitions, income support, and collaboration between public and private sectors'.[22]

Make best use of technology

The great hope in making education affordable at scale is the role of online digital courses. Take Coursera's iMBA offering with the University of Illinois at Urbana-Champaign which costs $22,000 – that's a third of the cost of a resident MBA at the same university. However, despite the initial growth, to date the development of online degrees has been cautious and mainly restricted to masters-level programmes. It seems that, far from reducing costs, most universities have experienced substantial increases as they are now required to produce both digital and traditional materials.

Over the coming decades we can expect further investment in online courses. That is in part because their digital foundation has elements that classroom-based teaching lacks. Digital courses offer potential educational advantages from the 'gamification' of learning (that is, making learning fun by combining teaching and evaluation through a similar experiential process as computer gaming); a greater degree of personalisation; and, through 'big data', the potential to provide great insight into what pedagogically works well.

Yet while technology holds enormous potential for reforming education, it's important to bear in mind the words of American sociologist Tressie McMillan Cottom: 'If you believe technology is the answer to everything that plagues higher education, you probably don't understand technology or higher education.'[23]

Take the challenges that technology-based learning company Udacity experienced when they collaborated with the San José State University (SJSU). The aim of the collaborations was to provide three courses, in mathematics and remedial and entry-level statistics, to a mix of students at SJSU and community colleges. In a follow-up study, the learning outcomes of students on the Udacity course were compared with those in traditional face-to-face education. The pass rate for the face-to-face group was around 80 per cent – for the online group it was less than 30 per cent.

Of course, this does not mean that online courses are hopelessly flawed, or that they cannot improve over time. There is no doubt that the reasons for their disappointing performance can be understood and improved upon. What was clear in this instance was that for this mix of students there were real barriers to learning: some lacked constant access to a computer or device; some had problems of combining learning with other demands; and some had difficulty building on their existing levels of knowledge. All these challenges signal that simply relying on technology alone will not solve the challenge of providing lifelong learning. Technology is certainly a powerful tool: the ability to take short online courses gives Estelle new options that help her learn in a much more flexible manner. But the challenges she faces in acquiring new skills go beyond just flexible learning.

A NEW EDUCATION SYSTEM

Education systems are already undergoing a process of change, but they are at the early stages. In part this reflects the traditional focus of higher education institutions on those students aged 18–21. The shift has to be towards the institutions that are able to support lifelong learning and focus on the needs and motivations of older students. The potential institutional gains are huge given the relative size of the markets. Take the UK, where there are currently 4.2 million people in the traditional educational age range of 20–24, but more than 46 million in the lifelong learning range of 25 and over. Or Japan where there are only 6.3 million people in the traditional education range, but more than 73 million in the lifelong learning range of 25–70.

Already the implications of these demographics are being felt. In 2018 the Harvard Extension School admitted more students than the rest of Harvard put together. Given the enormous commercial opportunity this represents, it is no surprise that investors are making big bets. In 2010 around $0.7 billion was invested in education by venture capital funds. By 2018 that had risen to $7 billion. Moreover, by 2018, according to Michael Moe, co-founder of education investors GSV Asset Management, eight 'unicorns' (tech start-ups who achieve a $1 billion valuation) had been created.

But beyond these investment figures is one of the most significant requirements for social ingenuity. Society desperately needs a dynamic process of lifelong learning which has both breadth and inclusivity. In the words of Harvard Extension School dean Huntington Lambert: 'My single passion now is to drive all of us continuing-education providers to serve the 20 million people in the US who need to be re-educated to participate in the knowledge economy, and their two billion global peers.'[24]

The scope of the agenda is extraordinary.

8

THE GOVERNMENT AGENDA

Governments have a driving role to play in our quest for human flourishing; they need to act now – by providing platforms that enable and encourage everyone to act as social pioneers; and by providing insurance and support to those who are adversely impacted during this transition.

This role is critical because governments possess powers to bring about change that no other institution has: to tax, to create subsidies and benefits, to legislate, regulate and coordinate. While the agenda for governments is inevitably wide, here our focus is on those elements we have explored throughout the book: work, careers, education and relationships.

In considering these elements it is clear that the foundations underpinning current government policy are out of date. Too much policy is based on the assumption of a three-stage and a seventy-year-long life; that the key assets of firms are physical capital, such as machinery and real estate; and that most careers are spent in full-time employment anchored to a specific firm. Government policy must instead address the reality of a multistaged hundred-year life where a firm's value is derived from intangible rather than tangible assets, and where a substantial part of work will be in flexible jobs This will involve rewiring existing institutions, policies and regulations in order to minimise the potential bad outcomes and support good outcomes.

In order to minimise bad outcomes, governments have to ensure that everyone understands the imperative of preparing and investing for their future. This is challenging because for the last few decades substantial amounts of risk have been transferred from governments and firms onto individuals. Consider the risks associated with longevity. In most countries, state pensions have become less generous, while at the same time the defined benefit (DB) pension schemes of corporations have declined in number. That means people have to rely more on their own savings to support them through what could be a potentially very long retirement. Or consider the risks associated with technological change. At a time of significant transition, the responsibility for training has shifted from the government and corporations to employees, so that if people don't invest in their education, the chances of losing their job are high. Finally, consider the risks associated with work: where previously a stable full-time job could be counted on to provide some level of income security, the variable work schedule of the gig economy will no longer provide this. This risk transfer from governments to individuals puts a real premium on governments to ensure as many people as possible are made aware of the need to prepare.

Minimising bad outcomes is crucial, but it's also the role of governments to support good outcomes. They can do this by creating a narrative about the future that supports people like Estelle, Tom and Ying to navigate the crossroads in their working life. These labour market and skills insights would help them plan their next career step and ensure their learning is targeted to their being more productive and marketable. There is also a role here for governments to facilitate innovation: for instance, by designing regulations and legislation that enable people like Ying to work for longer and provide resources for people like Estelle to embark on lifelong learning.

AVOIDING BAD OUTCOMES

All of us face a variety of risks in our everyday life. You may, for example, worry about a house fire, in which case you can mitigate this risk by fitting smoke detectors and taking out an insurance policy. But in facing the uncertain future created by technology and longevity, you are challenged by the speed, magnitude and unpredictability of the likely changes ahead. Given that you cannot know the ultimate impact of technology on employment, or the path of future longevity gains, these risks are hard to deal with. And, unlike house insurance, there is no simple policy that can be bought that covers you against them. The likely scale and number of people affected makes this a significant agenda for governments, who need to provide protection against the major risks of unemployment, bad jobs, financial insecurity and bad health.

Insure the person – *not the* job

Governments could act to protect workers by shielding them from the impact of technological change, for example, by introducing regulation that slows the introduction of new technologies. In the case of new mobility platforms, they could intervene on behalf of incumbents, such as taxi drivers, or impose tougher safety standards that slow the roll out of autonomous trucks. Or governments could introduce regulations that prevent firms from laying off workers without government permission, or legislate that firms pay a substantial tax for every redundancy.

On the face of it, protecting jobs sounds like a positive way of reducing risk. But it comes with problems. Most importantly, regulating against new technologies tends to stop the spread of higher productivity through the economy. This in turn prevents consumers from benefiting from lower prices and new products and runs the risk of trapping the economy into a low wage–low productivity trap. In addition, by making it harder to *fire* workers, the knock-on effect is that it makes firms reluctant to *hire* them. This can even lead to an increase in unemployment if the effect on hiring is strong enough. If governments want to maintain employment in the face of technological change, they must do all they can to encourage *job creation* rather than focus on stopping *job destruction*.

This is the emphasis of the Danish government's 'flexicurity' model, in which hiring and firing is equally easy: unemployed workers receive significant benefits plus access to education, whilst

185

retraining programmes successfully achieve re-employment. In other words, the approach is to protect the worker rather than the job. This combination helps support the productivity gains from new technologies and the transition to a high wage economy. It also actively supports worker welfare during the transition. Only if the pace of job loss from technological change is overwhelmingly rapid should policies be used to slow the tide.

Avoiding inequality

Rising inequality has become a growing political problem in many countries and this looks set to continue. According to one study based on German data, there is a strong inverse correlation between a worker's education and the risk of them losing their job from automation. More than half of jobs that require no vocational training have a 70 per cent chance or more of being lost through automation, compared to only 15 per cent of the jobs occupied by university graduates.[1] Those with the fewest resources and least slack are the most likely to experience reluctant transitions as their work is automated. How can governments help people such as Estelle?

One policy which is receiving attention is a universal basic income (UBI). A number of governments, including those of the US, Finland, Kenya, the Netherlands and Switzerland, have all experimented with small scale UBI projects. In its purest form, a UBI is a fixed sum of money that everyone in society receives irrespective of their age, wealth, or whether they are employed. In other words, it's a citizen's income for people to spend in any way they choose and set at a level substantial enough to live on without working. Advocates of UBI argue that it is a guaranteed way of preserving the standard of living in response to a 'robot apocalypse'. It's also potentially a simpler system than the current patchwork of schemes and offers fewer disincentives while achieving universal coverage.

For some, UBI is not just a means of insuring those who lose their job; it is a way of liberating humans to focus on something more purposeful. By providing a guaranteed income it could help unlock entrepreneurial talents amongst the entire population, not just those with the resources to take risks. Estelle could finally focus on the training she needs to qualify as a beautician and set about starting her own beauty salon. Freed from the need to earn, communities would benefit from ever more voluntary work and investment. In other words, UBI could support a more fulfilling version of work.

The critics of UBI focus on less positive features of human behaviour. They worry how people will respond to a guaranteed income – will they become reluctant to seek any form of work, whether paid or unpaid? Of course, if UBI is a response to a world where technology has taken away all jobs, these disincentive effects are immaterial. However, in a world where employment still exists, a key issue is whether the disincentive effects of UBI are greater than those of the current system.

There are also concerns about the cost of UBI. Because of its universal nature it is expensive and not necessarily focused on those with the greatest needs. In its purest form, UBI replaces all existing social security schemes (e.g. unemployment benefit, social credit, pensions, tax allowances) so the cost is offset against these fiscal savings. That means that the overall cost of UBI then depends on how well targeted a country's existing benefits are.[2] In some countries the introduction of UBI is estimated to be costly[3] – around £44 billion in the UK and €2.7 billion in France; in others it would save money, in Italy around €41billion and €1.5 billion in Finland.

A more pressing challenge is the how UBI can support those experiencing employment transitions. Here the results are mixed. In 2019, the Finnish government concluded a two-year pilot involving 2,000 unemployed people. By the end participants felt healthier, more confident, relaxed, and appreciative of the less bureaucratic and intrusive nature of basic income. But UBI made no difference to their likelihood of finding employment. It neither sharpened motivation nor blunted incentives compared to other social security schemes.

Whatever social insurance scheme is implemented, it crucially needs to both support people in their transitions *and* increase the likelihood of new jobs being created. This requires providing training and education support for workers during any period of unemployment, while making income support convertible into a wage subsidy if and when they are subsequently re-employed. In supporting job creation, it is important that governments recognise the broadening concept of work and that job creation can be wider than formal employment. Therefore, social security should also be convertible into a start-up subsidy, in the case of self-employment, while encouraging community work and social entrepreneurship will be important in areas of unemployment.

There is another way in which governments can boost job creation. Education and reskilling will undoubtedly play a key role in supporting people to become more employable, but if the growing demand for workers is in high-skilled occupations, then this will be a stretch for many. So there is a role here for government in supporting jobs in those small- and medium-sized enterprises that are likely to be less prone to automation and demand a mixture of human skills. This means that government industrial policy must be focused on not only supporting technological giants, but also small-scale entrepreneurs. In other words, policies that help Estelle set up her own beauty salon will be an important means of maintaining employment during the transition.

Protect against 'bad jobs'

It is possible that more people will be employed in contingent work and this creates employment that is more precarious and more likely to take place in the gig economy as contractors or freelancers. This can be good work: Radhika loves the autonomy and freedom that working as a freelancer brings. But for many others (and perhaps for Radhika in the future) on zero-hours contracts, the lack of certainty and corporate support can be a real source of risk and stress. Many of these new jobs provide no training, no pension contribution, no vacation or sickness pay. This can add to the sense of insecurity and lack of preparedness for the future.

Should governments pick up the obligation by providing tax incentives for contingent workers to contribute to their own pension, education needs and health care? Alternatively, should they introduce employment legislation that forces firms to extend their obligations across a broader range of jobs? The courts are already playing a role here. In a landmark decision in December 2018, a UK court upheld the case brought by the Independent Workers Union of Great Britain (IWGB). They ruled that Uber had unlawfully classified Uber drivers as independent contractors rather than workers. By doing so they had denied them their basic rights such as a guaranteed minimum wage and holiday pay. We can expect more of these legal representations to follow.

We have throughout this book made the case for the crucial role of flexible working, as people across a long working life strive to balance work with other commitments such as children, elderly parents, learning and recharging. Some firms who value their workers will include flexibility as part of the deal. But others will not. Also on the agenda then will be the issue of whether governments should introduce more general 'right to request' legislation, in the case, for example, of paternity leave or parental caring.

Finally, it is important to recognise that technology is not destiny in terms of the balance between good or bad jobs. We believe that government policy must support workers upskilling and reskilling when they are faced with technological transitions. This encourages firms to direct technology investment towards *augmenting* human skills rather than *replacing* them. In contrast, a poorly educated workforce and generous tax write-offs for capital investment will simply encourage firms to use ineffective AI to substitute for labour, not because it is technically adept but rather because it is cheaper. This scenario will offer only frustration to the consumer and poor employment outcomes.

Through minimum wages, workplace safety regulations and similar protective measures, government policy can help influence the number of 'good' jobs created. In the words of MIT professor Daron Acemoglu: 'Such measures are often blamed for choking off employment. But they can actually create a virtuous cycle of growth, because the cost floor for labour creates an incentive for firms to rationalise and upgrade their production processes, thereby increasing productivity and thus demand. Similarly, by ensuring that product markets remain competitive, governments can prevent firms from charging monopoly prices and reaping higher profits without having to hire more workers.'[4]

Protect against bad financial outcomes

There are real risks ahead for those who have not prepared sufficiently. Specifically, a longer life increases the risk of outliving savings. The insurance market has already created a way of mitigating this risk in the form of annuities whereby an individual makes a lump sum investment and an insurance company then pays them a fixed amount of income for the rest of their life regardless of how long they live. This of course assumes they have a lump sum to invest, but there is also another challenge. This type of insurance is vulnerable to adverse selection. Simply put, those who imagine they will live longer are much more likely to take out an annuity than those who believe they only have a few years ahead of them. As a result, when firms price the cost of buying an annuity they do so assuming the customer has above average health. The result is that the payout rate on an annuity is unattractive for many people.[5]

People are also now more exposed to the risks of longevity because of the decline in defined benefit (DB) company pensions. These are pensions provided by the employer who pay a fixed annual pension for life depending on length of service and salary. As life expectancy increased, these became expensive and so most companies dropped them, replacing them with defined contribution (DC) pensions. In these the pension amount depends on the value of the investment made by the individual and the employer, the performance of the financial market and the length of life. This switch to DC schemes puts more emphasis on an individual's actions and efforts and exposes them to greater longevity risk. One way that governments can reduce this risk is through social security benefits in retirement. However, the

190

higher an individual's income, the smaller the insurance provided by social security. This suggests that governments need to provide greater tax incentives for individuals to hold more of their pensions in the form of annuities.

Governments can also help by encouraging people to save more. In the US, the National Institute on Retirement Security estimates that the median retirement savings of Americans between the ages of 55–64 is zero. Even for those who do have a retirement account, the average balance is only $88,000. At current interest rates, that would provide an annual income of less than $2,000.

A positive step to boosting retirement savings has been pension automatic enrolment, which was introduced in 1992 by the Australian government. Auto-enrolment mandates all employers to contribute a minimum of 3 per cent into an employee's pension pot (superannuation guarantee fund, or 'Supers'). Over time, this contribution rate has increased and is scheduled to reach 9 per cent by 2019. Supers work because they use a behavioural 'nudge'. Persuading people to save and contribute to a savings scheme is difficult; the power of auto-enrolment is that people 'opt out' rather than 'opt in'. Just as people tend not to make an active decision to join a pension scheme, so they tend not to take an active decision to opt out of it. Whilst auto-enrolment is relatively easily implemented for employees, this is again where the changing architecture of the labour market is causing problems. How can such schemes be extended to cover the more exposed contingent workforce?

There is also the challenge of living for longer but being incapacitated at an early age. Imagine being diagnosed with dementia at the age of sixty and then living to ninety. This puts an enormous financial and emotional burden on the individual and their family. Who bears the cost of this risk? It seems reasonable to expect people to save for some level of care, but is it reasonable to assume they save enough to finance a very lengthy and expensive care period? This is an issue of rising importance for governments. In the UK in 2011, the government commissioned the Dilnot Report. This recommended a ceiling of £35,000 for an individual's lifetime contribution to their own social care costs and that social care would be subject to means testing so that people with low incomes would not have to contribute, with an individual's contribution rising depending on their wealth. Providing social insurance to cover these 'tail' risks is important given the diversity in how people age.

Reduce bad health outcomes

Clive worries about his long-term health (morbidity) and is especially concerned about a long period of ill health at the end of his life. He knows that whilst he will probably live longer than his father, these extra years may not all be healthy. The good news for Clive is that a study of 195 countries for the period 1990–2015 showed 'the *proportion* of lifespans spent in ill health has remained comparatively constant since 1990'.[6] Given that the majority of life is healthy, this implies that the majority of *extra* years of life are also healthy. Yet whilst the *proportion* of lifespan spent in ill health is not rising, the *actual number* of years of ill health is. Think of it this way: if 70 per cent of your lifespan is healthy, then an increase in life expectancy of ten years equates to an added seven years of good health, but an added three years of poor health.

A priority for governments has to be to compress this period of morbidity[7] and reduce the years spent at the end of life in ill health. That is important to people like Clive; it is also important in combating the dramatic rise in health costs we showed in Figure 1.3. This means focusing on what Jay Olshansky of the University of Illinois at Chicago calls the 'red zone' – the time at the end of life characterised by frailty and disease.[8]

One way of doing this is to take into account the *malleability* of age – to recognise that the process of aging is not fixed. The health costs shown in Figure 1.3 raise the anxiety that, as a society ages, so health costs must inevitably rise. But that is to fall for what has been termed the 'red herring effect'[9] – in other words to view chronological age as the key predictor of health. This distracts from what really matters for health: biological age. It seems to us that governments should now focus on how the process of aging can be improved and so reduce the impact of an aging society on health expenditure and government debt.

How might this be achieved? From a technological perspective, it would be wise to support and fund aging research, adding to the $140 billion investment that investors and corporations such as Google's biotech company, Calico, are making. As Olshansky remarks: 'If you can slow the biological process of aging, even a minor slowdown in the rate at which we age yields improvements in virtually every condition of frailty and disability and mortality.'[10] Aging research could unlock the biological aging process.

But for now, the most significant impact would be to switch the focus of the health system away from *intervention* in ill health towards *preventative* measures that prolong healthy lifespan. That's challenging because, traditionally, health systems were designed to treat young populations; to intervene when young people fall ill, often through intensive bed-based treatments. This may make sense when the population is young, but as the population ages and the disease burden shifts towards non-communicable illnesses this is expensive and inefficient. What is needed is to move away from what UK Minister of Health, Matt Hancock, calls the national *hospital* system towards a national *health* system. That means gearing the health service towards supporting people to maintain their independence, slowing down the incidence of co-morbidities, and helping them manage and live with this if they occur. In other words, a focus on wellness rather than illness.

Realising this change will also require a shift in ageist assumptions. There is evidence that older people tend to receive fewer medical resources when it comes to preventative medicine. Somewhat paradoxically, if the medical costs of aging are to be contained, then the delivery of medical resources has to be age-blind. Denying medical treatment to older patients reflects a lack of awareness of the malleability of age. The rate at which health expenditure rises with age is not fixed but can be reduced by interventions at all ages, including old age.

Technological ingenuity is already at work developing better preventative practices. Government health systems are awash with data which offer a fertile training ground for algorithms to learn from and provide better predictive insights. When combined with biomarkers that track an individual's health, the hope is that preventative health care will target specific health issues. And when AI offers home-based diagnoses and contact with doctors and hospital specialists, then the frequent monitoring of health becomes a reality.

Whilst advances in technology hold much promise, the most important way to influence preventative health currently is rather more rudimentary but no less powerful as a consequence. In the words of anti-aging expert Eric Verdin, president and CEO of the Buck Institute for Research on Aging: 'Exercise and nutrition are likely to be the best interventions [for aging] that we will have for a long time to come.'[11]

Governments have already stepped in here by using taxation to reduce tobacco and alcohol consumption. They are now turning their attention to sugar. In 2011, Hungary was the first country to introduce a sugar tax and has since been followed by a number of countries, including France, the UK, Saudi Arabia, Thailand and notably Mexico, where 70 per cent of the population are estimated to be obese.

Encouraging citizens to keep fit and active will inevitably rise higher on government agendas. The need is clear when about one-third of Europeans are not sufficiently physically active, and this is estimated to contribute annually to 10 per cent of deaths through raised levels of heart disease, diabetes and colon cancer.[12] Some local governments are stepping up – for example working with urban planners to ensure that their cities are more appealing to pedestrians and cyclists, enhancing and creating more public spaces and building easier routes through towns.

PROMOTING GOOD OUTCOMES

There are three central issues that governments should consider in promoting good outcomes: providing a pathway for the acquisition of future skills; supporting healthy aging; and creating a longevity economy.

Governments are expecting citizens to navigate their own working lives. But in order to do so, workers need insight about what could happen to their current job, and in making plans they need awareness of which jobs will be more valuable in the future. Clearly, educational institutions and corporates have a role to play here. Our concern though is their insights will be partial and biased, thus opening up an important role for governments. They can fulfil this role by collating data from a variety of sources and stakeholders (schools and universities, trainers, recruitment agencies, employers and job centres) and effecting important public good by mapping the current and future demand for specific jobs and skills. The German Federal Ministry of Labour and Social Affairs, for example, has done this through a two-year multi-stakeholder dialogue about the 2030 future of work.

Building this map of current and future job and skills demands is important, but the real challenge is getting this information to the people who most need it. The German ministry made this a priority. First they partnered with the various training skills providers to share with them their future skills data so they could orientate their curriculum towards these needs. Next, they disseminated the skill maps to citizens through the German network of employment services, who used them to counsel people about their job prospects and how they can adapt. Finally, they worked closely with companies and their work councils to encourage them to create innovative spaces to try out new ways to work and learn.

In the UK the government-sponsored innovation foundation Nesta is running an 'Open Jobs' project. This encourages job seekers in a specific city or sector to access a local map of real-time job adverts while exploring the future prospects of different skills and jobs out to 2030. The aspiration is that both companies and educational institutions will have access to future job information and will design and provide upskilling programmes accordingly. Given access to this, Estelle could see if her fears about automation and the cashier jobs she does are valid, and it could give her impetus to train as a beautician.

In creating these initiatives, the balance between national and local projects will be crucial. While there is much for national governments to do, expect ever more innovation and social entrepreneurship at city, town or regional level. That is in part because the impact of longevity and technology will vary substantially from place to place, which means that national policies alone will not be sufficient. But it is more than this: local initiatives also give more space to social pioneers to experiment and understand what really works in their community.

Promote healthy aging

There is much that governments can do to reduce bad health outcomes, particularly in the way that health and medical interventions are delivered. A significant theme in this book has been that aging is *recursive*. Today's young are the future old and how they behave today influences how they will age in the future. And whilst about a quarter of the variance in health in older age is genetically determined, the rest is strongly affected by the cumulative effect of health behaviours and inequities across the life course.[13] This is clearly a government agenda and a debate that goes beyond health, medicine and exercise. It embraces the impact on current and future health of air pollution, stressful jobs and financial anxiety, loneliness and poor relationships.

There is also much that governments can do to take a positive lead in counterbalancing much of the pessimism about an aging society. That is happening in Japan where Prime Minister Abe in 2017 set up the 'Council for Designing a 100-Year Life Society'. This aimed to create a dialogue between key stakeholders (ministers, trade unions, educators) and raise citizens' awareness about how they could invest in their longer futures. The council also crafted a range of policy solutions designed to support those changes.

It is also important that governments are more realistic about longevity data. That is because current government communications about life expectancy data encourages people to underestimate how long they may live, and therefore to underprepare. The reason is that when governments predict life expectancy, they focus on *period* measures of life expectancy. In the UK, for example, the result is that current government calculations of period measures of average life expectancy at birth is 79.2 for men and 82.9 for women. These government longevity figures are important – they are discussed in the press and given prominence in government publications. They become the figures most citizens are aware of. But they are not the most appropriate figures; an alternative *cohort* measure is much more useful. This puts current life expectancy in the UK at 92.2 for women and 89.6 for men; in other words people would be preparing now for an extra ten years of life.

Why the difference? Period measures of life expectancy assume that a child born in 2019 lives their entire life medically in 2019 – so when they reach the age of sixty-five in 2084, their chance of surviving to sixty-six is the same as a sixty-five-year-old in 2019. Given the history of medical progress, this is a conservative assumption. By contrast, the cohort measures try to factor in improvements in mortality and therefore take into account that a sixty-five-year-old in 2084 should have a better chance of reaching sixty-six than a sixty-five-year-old today. If governments are to create a narrative of healthy aging, they must place more focus on cohort measures of life expectancy. The danger of not doing so is that citizens fail to take the long view and as a consequence underinvest in their own future.

Create a longevity economy

The more governments succeed in supporting healthy longer lives, the more important the goal of creating a 'longevity economy' becomes. This would ensure that the economy grows (rather than declines) in response to longer, more productive lives. To achieve this means rewiring institutions and policies so that people don't just live longer but are able to be productive for longer. There is a real challenge here – currently the foundation of much government policy is chronological age and the assumptions of a three-stage life. That leads inevitably to 'age stickiness' – by sticking to chronological measures of age, the economy fails to reap the benefits of improvements in biological age.

Creating a longevity economy starts with getting the right measures and data. One of the most central measures used to describe an aging society is the old-age dependency ratio (OADR). This is the ratio of the number of people aged over sixty-five (the historically assumed age of retirement) to those of working age (those aged 16–64). It is a crude measure of how many pensioners (people over the age of sixty-five) each working person will have to support.

Globally this ratio is currently around 0.25 – one pensioner for every four workers. By 2100 it will reach 0.5 and in some advanced economies (e.g. Japan) it will reach one – that's one pensioner supported by every worker. These increasing dependency ratios are at the heart of the aging society narrative and the fears of inevitably slowing economic growth and rising government debt.

We believe it is time to reject this ratio as an economic tool. Our argument is threefold. First, it assumes that everyone under sixty-five works and everyone over sixty-five does not: this is clearly inaccurate. Next, the notion of the old being 'dependent' on the young is misleading as it fails to recognise the growing dependence of job creation on the economic power of the 'silver dollar', the expenditure of older people. Third, it fails to capture the natural cycle of dependency within society – the current old previously paid the taxes to finance the education and health care of those currently working. These are important issues, for by assuming those aged over sixty-five are dependent on the young, the OADR fuels intergenerational conflict rather than recognising the more complex intergenerational compact at work.

But there is a more fundamental issue: the definition of 'old' as people aged over sixty-five. As we have argued, this chronological approach completely misses the concept of the malleability of age and so denies the existence of a longevity economy. To understand the implications of this concept we need to take into consideration 'age inflation' – that chronological age is adjusted for improvements in biological age. If we make this adjustment (by defining 'old' as having the same mortality rate as a sixty-five-year-old in 1950) then for the US, for example, there is a rather different picture for the dependency ratio. We present this in Figure 8.1. Using the traditional definition of old as sixty-five years or above, then the OADR increases over time – it's a narrative of an economy under pressure from fewer workers, higher pensions and higher health costs. However, if instead we adjust for age inflation, the dependency rate declines – the narrative becomes one of a population aging better and an increase in the potential labour force. Surely that's good, not bad, news for the economy.

There is a substantial macroeconomic impact of increasing the proportion of people working over the age of sixty-five. In the UK, it is estimated that every one-year increase in the age of retirement leads to a 1 per cent increase in GDP.[14] If people are healthier and productive for longer, this should boost the economy and the effects will be sizeable if supported by appropriate policies.

In order to seize this advantage of the longevity economy, it is imperative that governments do whatever they can to encourage

FIGURE 8.1 Old-age dependency ratio: traditional and adjusted for age inflation

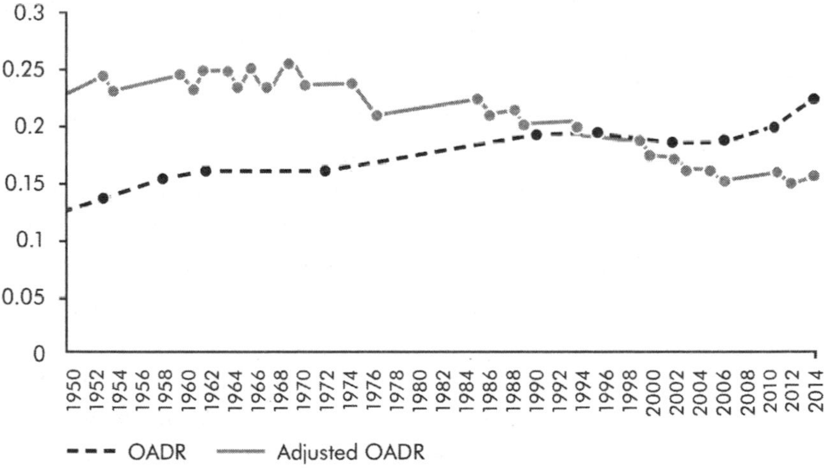

- - - OADR   —— Adjusted OADR

(source: authors' calculations)

and support people to work longer. An obvious step, and one that many governments have already taken, is to push back the age of retirement. But that's not going to be enough. The presence of 'age stickiness' is extensive and isn't just restricted to retirement but a host of other government and corporate practices such as health policies and education. There is real danger that if governments raise the retirement age without taking additional measures to boost productivity, this will simply lead to more unemployed older people. Raising retirement age has to be done in conjunction with a wider set of policies aimed at supporting not just longer careers, but longer and productive ones.

Government policy has also to acknowledge there are considerable inequalities in life expectancy, and not everyone is experiencing better health as they age. As a consequence, substantial increases in retirement age could effectively eliminate retirement for some. Governments have to ensure that the tax and benefit systems work together to provide incentives for those who can work for longer, while at the same time enabling those in ill health to retire on a reasonable income. Offering higher state pensions the longer a person chooses to work (as the Japanese government has done) could help make retirement the 'warm bath' that people want, rather than the 'cold shower' it tends to be now.

A common objection to government policies aimed at supporting the over-65s to work is the fear that it will take jobs away from the young. On the face of it this makes sense, but the reality is rather different. To understand how the economy could adjust to an influx of over-60s into the job market, consider the twentieth-century case of the increase in the number of women in the workforce. In the US in 1950, only 34 per cent of women aged over fifteen were in the workforce (17 million); by 2017 this had reached 57 per cent (71 million). These jobs were not taken from men – male employment rose by 41 million jobs over the same period.

How did the US create so many new jobs so that more women working didn't come at the expense of men? As more women worked, households earned more money and so spent more and as a result, the output of the US economy increased which led to the demand for more jobs. We can expect a similar cycle when more over sixty-five-year-olds work – they would earn more, spend more and this will ultimately stimulate the economy. There isn't a fixed amount of jobs to be allocated so in the aggregate there isn't an intergenerational conflict over jobs.

We can play out the implications of people over the age of sixty-five working by looking at the US economy. Only 27 per cent of people aged 65–74 currently work – that's compared to 64 per cent of those aged 55–64. So the question is: how many jobs would need to be created if by 2050 the proportion of those working aged 65–74 was the same as those aged 55–64 today?

Looking forward to 2050 there are expected to be 39 million Americans between the ages of 65–74. If 64 per cent of them want to work, that's 25 million jobs, and an increase of 17.5 million jobs than are currently accounted for by this age group. To accommodate this increase, the economy would need to create just over half a million jobs a year between now and 2050. That may sound a lot, but that's a lot less than the number of new jobs needed to be created when women entered the workforce. It is also lower than the recent rate of job creation in the US, which since 2000 has on average created 975,000 jobs each year. Accommodating the longevity economy will not require anything exceptional in the labour market.

AN INCLUSIVE AGENDA

For society to successfully shape its future to benefit from technology and longevity, a multiplicity of voices needs to be heard. There is a real danger that how these new technologies are used will be driven by the financial concerns of companies, or that responses to longevity will be solely led by governments and their worry over aging and public finances. Social ingenuity needs our collective individual voices if it is to succeed.

Throughout this book we have emphasised the need for self-reliance in preparing for the future. We have also discussed the obligations that governments and corporates have to us as individuals. However, the deepest web of rights and obligations are those that exist between us as individuals in our broader community. Looking back to the Industrial Revolution, trade unions and the labour movement played a key role in representing local communities and the needs of workers, and charities and friendly societies were significant campaigning forces. These social movements were not just advocacy groups, they were membership societies that either imposed or expected reciprocal support and obligations from amongst their members. It is crucial that similar social movements arise in the twenty-first century to help shape and amplify the narrative of governments.

Thinking beyond GDP

The narrative of governments is determined in part by what is measured and how these measures are described. That is why we have emphasised changes in how governments predict life expectancy (by using cohort rather than period measures) and old-age dependency ratios (by adjusting for age inflation).

However, the measure that gets the most attention is Gross Domestic Product (GDP), a concept first formally defined by Harvard's Simon Kuznets in 1934.[15] For most citizens, this is a measure they are familiar with, and rises and falls in GDP are taken as a proxy for the success of society. GDP is a measure of the total output of goods and services produced within the economy and, not surprisingly, it is both widely used and almost as widely criticised and misunderstood. Criticisms concern both the sins of commission (how GDP doesn't measure well what it intends to measure) as well as sins of omission (how GDP doesn't measure what really matters to us).

Should governments make use of other variables, such as the welfare and happiness of citizens, as an alternative measure to guide policy? The United Arab Emirates has appointed a Minister for Happiness and in 2018 the New Zealand finance minister, Grant Robertson, delivered the country's first 'well-being' budget. In his budget speech, Robertson noted that a 'focus on lifting well-being will require a different approach and different measures of success ... We want to take a broader view of success and move beyond simple measures such as GDP, which, while an important measure of economic output, does not tell the full story of peoples' well-being.'[16]

These are crucial issues. It seems to us that during these periods of transition that we have described, it is even more important to get the measures and the narrative right. Of course, as a steer to economic and fiscal policy, GDP and employment data will continue to be important. But as 'Engel's pause' describes, increases in GDP do not necessarily translate into improvements for individuals. In order to capture the experiences of individuals and to create a more accurate narrative, governments must adopt broader measures to assess how policies are helping people through the transition. These broader measures need to include the psychological and social costs of transitions so as to better understand how people and communities are being impacted.

These psychological and social costs include the balance between good and bad jobs, whether people are voluntarily moving into the contingent workforce or whether it is a last resort. These social indicators could also measure the integrity and vibrancy of the local community. In other words, governments need to target the quality of the transition as well as the ultimate size of the economy.

Rewiring the political system

Technology is fundamentally reshaping concepts such as 'labour' and 'capital', and this in turn means governments need to find new ways to tax, redistribute and regulate. Take the concept of employment. Historically a major cause of poverty was not having a job – either through unemployment or being out of work. In response to this, many countries developed welfare systems based on whether people were working or not. However, the link between poverty and unemployment has become more complex with the gig economy. Estelle has a job but a low wage and variable hours means financially she frequently struggles.

The problem is, what does 'work' mean in the gig economy? Does the concept of a 'job' still make sense? And just as the concept of work and labour has changed, so too has the concept of capital: Uber claims it is not a transport company because it owns no modes of transport; Facebook says it is not a media company because it produces no media content; eBay and Alibaba are major retail sites that hold no inventory; Airbnb is valued at twice that of Hilton Hotels, but does not own or operate real estate. The value of these firms, and many more, are based on intangible capital (reflecting investment in brand, research and development, intellectual property and design) rather than tangible capital (factories, machines, offices and so on). These underlying shifts in what is capital, what is a job and how people work, is creating significant tension, as current tax and benefit systems no longer serve their purpose.

These shifts are also impacting the political process. That is in part because the delineation of political parties has historically been based on these traditional concepts of labour and capital. And as these concepts become a less effective way of describing our world, so these shifts are creating political turbulence as nontraditional parties and leaders emerge in response to the nonalignment of traditional parties with contemporary concerns.

Longevity is also putting pressure on democratic institutions. As society ages and people live for longer, society has to reconsider whose voices are being heard. If people are preparing for a much longer future, should the voices of the young be heard to counterbalance the voices of the old? That is the view of Cambridge University's David Runciman, who argues that people from the age of six should be able to participate in voting. Without this, he believes, an aging society is set to bring about a democratic crisis and a bias against governments with long-term plans. As he points out, the inverted age pyramid in most societies means that eighteen-year-olds are significantly outnumbered by the old, who can vote right through their lives.

It seems to us that imagining that older people are less forward-looking than six-year-olds is an ageist assumption. But he's got a point. This concern about intergenerational equity is surely valid in a world that needs to be changed to deal with longevity and new technologies. The changes that need to be made now will affect the young for a great deal longer than they will affect the old – so it's crucial that their voices are heard.

All of us are having to redesign life and our society, and we need to ensure that generations can come together to sculpt a more human future.

Throughout this book we have described the crucial role for individuals of exploring and pioneering. This role is also crucial for governments. We need both social *and* governmental ingenuity if we are to succeed in this transition and respond positively to the changes created by technology and longevity.

POSTSCRIPT: MOVING FORWARD

We are all in the early stages of a profound shift in how individually and as a society we structure our lives and learn to flourish. In the years ahead we will hear about and, more to the point, witness ever more extraordinary examples of human ingenuity. There are sure to be fantastic new breakthroughs in AI and robotics, further improvements in how we age, more evidence of the impact of an aging society and an ever-greater variety in how we form families and communities.

If we are to prepare for the future, we all need to be insightful and curious about these developments. But ultimately it is about our actions: how we test our assumptions about how to flourish; how we enlist the courage to be social pioneers; and how we grasp the opportunities this extraordinary transition is creating.

The fact that institutions – be they governments, corporations or education – are lagging behind our aspirations is sure to be a source of frustration. But paradoxically, this under-institutionalisation creates a great deal of space for self-expression and for collective action. So, rather than look to institutions for a steer, it would make sense to continually scan society for interesting behavioural innovations. These emerging new ways of living will be crucial since inevitably we will all be thinking and acting differently from past generations. Indeed, if you are not thinking and acting differently, then it is unlikely that you are preparing yourself for this changed and changing world.

Our key message is that while the narrative of your life has become longer, the periods and stages that build this narrative have shortened in the wake of more transitions. Throughout this book we have described the consequences of this new long life. Together they point to five simple actions that you need to engage with.

Act pre-emptively. We are living through a period of profound change that will impact everyone. An ever-greater degree of responsibility for managing that change is being handed over to you, meaning that you must take action now.

Orientate yourself to the future. Whatever your age, you have a longer time horizon ahead of you than past generations. This puts a premium on being forward-looking and thinking carefully about investments that can compound over time.

Be aware of your possible selves. A longer life and more transitions open up a wider set of possible selves. Making the most of this will require exploring these possibilities and keeping your options open for longer.

Focus on malleability and recursivity. Both your age and how your time is structured and distributed have become more malleable. That means your actions now can influence how you age and your future options and choices.

Accept transitions. Whether under your instigation or forced upon you, substantive life changes can be difficult. Looking forward, these transitions will inevitably be more frequent and will form the knots that tie the threads of a multistage life together.

These are guidelines for individuals, but across your life, your capacity to flourish will fundamentally depend on your relationships with others. We cannot become social pioneers in isolation, and the strength and depth of our relationships with others will be crucial in providing coherence and security. These cannot be taken for granted and require making commitments and having trusting and open conversations.

But it goes beyond this. Both within our families and our communities we must forge and invest in intergenerational relationships and focus on embedding lifetime relationships across a longer and more transitional life. The focus is therefore on finding new ways to engage with our communities. This will be crucial because only collective voices will be heard by the institutions that shape our lives. Their need for social ingenuity is great and the agenda for change is crucial: without our collective voices they will continue to lag behind human aspirations.

We acknowledge that change will not be easy and the widening gap between technological and social ingenuity brings with it undoubted risks. However, we are being presented with extraordinary opportunities to live for longer and in ways that enable greater freedom and give more options. Being faced with new choices can be unsettling. But if we are able individually and socially to make wise choices, then we have the possibility of healthier, longer and more fulfilled lives. As social norms start to break down, the space created provides a wonderful opportunity to imagine the possibilities of the new long life.

In writing this book our hope was to support conversations about this new long life. Our website **www.thenewlonglife.com** has more information about the book, additional resources to help your own thinking and planning, and space to share your own stories and insights. We will continue to engage with these topics through our research, our teaching and writing, and our advisory work. You can keep up to date with these efforts on our personal websites **www.ProfAndrewJScott.com** and **www.lyndagratton. com**, as well as by following us on Twitter: **@ProfAndrewScott** and **@LyndaGratton**.

We wish you every success as you embark on your social pioneering and look forward to hearing from you as you move forward.

NOTES

Introduction

1 https://www.bbc.co.uk/news/world-us-canada-42170100.
2 https://www.bloomberg.com/graphics/2017-job-risk/.
3 https://www.newyorker.com/magazine/2019/05/20/can-we-live-longer-but-stay-younger.

Chapter One

1 In the words of Douglas Adams, author of *The Hitchhiker's Guide to the Galaxy* 'Technology is a word that describes something that doesn't work yet' https://www.azquotes.com/quote/343497
2 Specifically, that the number of transistors that could be held on an integrated circuit would double.
3 https://www.statista.com/statistics/499431/global-ip-data-traffic-forecast/.
4 Perhaps we can coin our own tongue-in-cheek 'Gratton–Scott' law: the number of 'laws' needed to explain technological progress grows exponentially with the hype a subject receives.
5 R. Baldwin, *The Globotics Upheaval: globalization, robotics and the future of work*, London: Weidenfeld and Nicolson, 2019.
6 'Jobs lost, jobs gained: workforce transitions in a time of automation'. McKinsey Global Institute, December 2017.
7 Although interestingly, after problems with hitting desired production targets through full automation, Musk noted: 'Yes, excessive automation at Tesla was a mistake. To be precise, my mistake. Humans are underrated.' https://www.cnbc.com/2018/04/13/elon-musk-admits-humans-are-sometimes-superior-to-robots.html
8 As with Elon Musk's alien dreadnought factory, the Henn-na hotel is another source of hubris, closing down in 2019. The robots could not do everything and required even more workers to perform tasks as well as attend to the robots.

9   Although robots cannot, of course, 'care' for you in an emotional sense.
10   A type of mathematical form which when fed data, adjusts its shape so as to mimic the real world (creating a form of numerical photo-copy of the original), enabling enhanced insight and decision-making.
11   D. Silver, J. Schrittwieser, K. Simonyan, I. Antonoglou, A. Huang, A. Guez, T. Hubert, L. Bakter, M. Lai, A. Bolton, Y. Chen, T. Lillicrap, F. Hui, L. Sifre, G. vanden Driessche, T. Graepel, D. Hassabis, 'Mastering the game of Go without human knowledge', *Nature*, 19 October 2017, Vol. 550, 354–9.
12   See https://www.npr.org/sections/money/2017/05/17/528807590/episode-606-spreadsheets?t=1533803451907.
13   As far back as the seventeenth century, Descartes was reflecting on this issue when he wrote: 'Even though such machines might do some things as well as we do them, or perhaps even better, they would inevitably fail in others, which would reveal they were acting not through understanding,' *Discourse on the Method*, 1637.
14   CAPTCHA stands for 'Completely Automated Public Turing test to tell Computers and Humans Apart', and are the online requests found on the web asking you to identify all the pictures which contain cars or other objects as a means of distinguishing humans from online bots.
15   M. Tegmark, *Life 3.0: Being Human in the Age of Artificial Intelligence*, London: Allen Lane, 2017, p. 42.
16   This is a *period* measure of life expectancy which effectively assumes that a Japanese girl born in 2018 lives their entire life in 2018, e.g. it assumes no further improvements in life expectancy occur over the next eighty-seven years. As such it is likely to under-estimate average life expectancy.
17   J. Oeppen, and J. Vaupel, 'Broken Limits to Life Expectancy', *Science*, May 2002, Vol. 296, 5570, 1029–31.
18   A. Case, and A. Deaton, 'Rising morbidity and mortality in mid-life among white non-Hispanic Americans in the 21st century', *Proceedings of the National Academy of Sciences in the United States of America*, Vol. 112, 49, 15078–83.
19   N. Kassebaum, et al, 'Global, regional and national disability adjusted life years for 315 diseases and injuries and healthy life expectancy, 1990–2015: A systematic analysis for the Global Burden of Disease Study 2015', *The Lancet*, 2016; Vol. 388, 10053, 1603–58.

20 A. Kingston, A. Comas-Herrera, and C. Jagger, 'Forecasting the care needs of the older population in England over the next 20 years: estimates from the Population Aging and Care Simulation (PACSim) modelling study', *The Lancet Public Health*, 2018; Vol. 3, 9, e447–55.

21 The injustice of inequality both within and across countries is apparent when realising that this statement does not apply to all children born today. The accident of where you are born has an enormous impact on life expectancy.

22 See, for instance, the Academy for Health and Lifespan Research: https://www.ahlresearch.org/vision.

23 David Sinclair, with Matthew D. LaPlante, *Lifespan: why we age and why we don't have to*, London: Thorson's, 2019; and A. Chalabi, and J. Mellon, *Juvenescence: Investing in the age of Longevity*, Douglas, Isle of Man: Fruitful Publications, 2017.

24 Anyone interested in longevity science will soon become extremely familiar with a 1mm roundworm called C.elegans whose genetic structure and short lifespan make it particularly suitable for study.

25 S. Harper, *How Population Change will Transform Our World*, Oxford: Oxford University Press, 2019.

26 All data from 'United Nations World Population Prospects, 2017', https://esa.un.org/unpd/wpp/DataQuery/

27 https://fullfact.org/economy/poverty-uk-guide-facts-and-figures/.

28 D. McCarthy, J. Sefton, and M. Weale, 'Generational Accounts for the United Kingdom', National Institute of Economic and Social Research Discussion Paper 377, January 2011, http://www.niesr. ac.uk/sites/default/files/publications/150311_171852.pdf.

CHAPTER TWO

1 A deeper understanding of liminality can be found in A. van Gennep et al, *The Rites of Passage*, Chicago: University of Chicago Press, 1960, and V. Turner, 'Betwixt and Between: The Liminal Period in Rites de Passage', in *The Forest of Symbols*, Ithaca: Cornell University Press, 1967.

2 http://www.bradford-delong.com/2014/05/estimates-of-world-gdp-one-million-bc-present-1998-my-view-as-of-1998-the-honest-broker-for-the-week-of-may-24-2014.html

3   M. Huberman, and C. Minns, 'The times they are not changin': days and hours of work in Old and New Worlds, 1870–2000', *Explorations in Economics History*, Vol. 44 (200710), 538–67.

4   W. Scheidel, *The Great Leveler: violence and the history of inequality from the Stone Age to the twenty-first century*, Princeton: Princeton University Press, 2018.

5   R. Chetty, M. Stepner, S. Abraham, S. Lin, B. Scuderi, N. Turner, A. Bergeron, D. Cutler, 'The association between income and life expectancy in the US', *Journal of American Medical Association*, 2016, Vol. 315 (20160426), 1750–66.

6   H. Markus, and P. Nunus, 'Possible Selves', *American Psychologist*, 1986, Vol. 4 (9), 954–69.

7   J. Panksepp, *Affective Neuroscience: the foundations of human and animal emotions*, New York: Oxford University Press, 1998.

8   D. Cable, *Alive at Work: the neuroscience of helping your people love what they do*, Boston: Harvard Business Review Press, 2018.

9   G. Vaillant, *Triumph of Experience*, Boston: Harvard University Press, 2012.

10 Garry Kasparov quoted in https://www.verdict.co.uk/garry-kasparov-humans-technology/ 'Garry Kasparov: We need better humans, not less technology', Verdict, Robert Scammell, 19 February 2019.

CHAPTER THREE

1   K. Thomas, 'Age and Authority in Early Modern England', London: British Academy, 1976.

2   P. Zweifel, S. Felder, and M. Meiers, 'Aging of population and health care expenditure: a red herring?', *Health Economics*, 1999, Vol. 8 (6) 485–96.

3   M. E. Levine, and E. M. Crimmins, 'Is 60 the new 50?: examining changes in biological age over the past two decades', *Demography*, 2018, 55, 2, 387–402.

4   J. B. Shoven, G. S. Goda, 'Adjusting government policies for age inflation', National Bureau of Economic Research (NBER), Working Paper, 14231, 2008.

5   J. Beard, and D. Bloom, 'Towards a comprehensive public health response to population aging', *The Lancet*, 2015; 385, 658–61.

6   B. Levy, et al, 'Longevity increased by positive self-perceptions of aging', *Journal of Personality and Social Psychology*, 2002; Vol. 83, 2, 261–70.

7   https://www.aging-better.org.uk/sites/default/files/2018-11/ELSA-analysis.pdf.

8   P. Thane, '*Old Age in English History*', Oxford: Oxford University Press, 2011.

9   https://www.youtube.com/watch?reload=9&v=lYdNjrUs4NM.

10 T. O'Donoghue, and M. Rabin, 'Doing it now or later', *American Economic Review*, Vol. 89, 1 March 1999, 103–24.

11 A discount rate is a basic concept in finance. If you are indifferent between $100 today and $110 in a year's time then your discount rate is 10 per cent, e.g. if you discount the $110 by 10 per cent you get $100 and the two are equivalent. The lower your discount rate the more patient you are. With a discount rate of 0 per cent you are indifferent between $100 today and $100 in a year's time – in other words you have the bird's-eye perspective.

12 C. Mogilner, H. E. Hershfield, J. Aaker, 'Rethinking time: implications for well-being', *Consumer Psychology Review*, 2018, Vol. 1, Issue 1, 41–53.

13 D. Blanchflower, and A. Oswald, 'Is well-being u-shaped over the life cycle?', *Social Science and Medicine*, 2008, Vol. 66 (8), 1733–49; see also J. Rauch, *The Happiness Curve*, New York: St Martin's Press, 2018.

14 J. Etkin, and C. Mogilner, 'Does variety among activities increase happiness?', *Journal of Consumer Research*, 2016, 43 (2), 210–29.

15 S. Mullainathan, and E. Shafir *Scarcity*, London: Penguin, 2014.

16 D. Kamerade, S. Wang, B. Burchell, S. Balderson, and A. Coutts, 'A shorter working week for everyone: how much paid work is needed for mental health and well-being?', *Social Science and Medicine*, 2019, in press 11253.

17 M. Aguiar, and E. Hurst, 'The increase in leisure inequality', NBER Working Paper, 13837, 2008.

18 H. E. Hershfield, C. Mogilner, and U. Barnea, 'People who choose time over money are happier', *Social Psychological and Personality Science*, 2016, Vol. 7 (7), 607–706.

19 https://www.nytimes.com/2016/09/11/opinion/sunday/what-should-you-choose-time-or-money.html.

20 McKinsey Global Institute, 'Jobs lost, jobs gained: workforce transitions in a time of automation', December 2017.

21 https://www.nytimes.com/2013/06/14/opinion/krugman-sympathy-for-the-luddites.html.

22 See C. Frey, *The Technology Trap: capital, labor, and power in the age of automation*, Princeton: Princeton University Press, 2019, for a historical analysis of how technology has throughout human history affected society and workers.

23 https://www.bls.gov/news.release/archives/jolts_03152019.htm.

24 https://www.bloomberg.com/news/articles/2018-08-01/how-a-trucking-shortage-is-fueling-u-s-inflation-quicktake.

25 McKinsey Digital. Chui, M.. Manyika, J. and Miremadi, M. 'Where machines could replace humans – and where they can't (yet)' July 2016.

26 http://www.pewresearch.org/wp-content/uploads/sites/9/2014/08/Future-of-AI-Robotics-and-Jobs.pdf.

27 https://economics.mit.edu/files/14641.

28 McKinsey Global Institute. Jobs lost, Jobs gained: Workforce transitions in a time of automation. December 2017.

29 J. E. Bessen, 'How computer automation affects occupations: technology, jobs and skills', Boston University School of Law, Law and Economics Research Paper, 2016, No. 15–4.

30 Bessen, 'How computer automation affects occupations'.

31 https://sloanreview.mit.edu/article/will-ai-create-as-many-jobs-as-it-eliminates/.

32 McKinsey Global Institute. Jobs lost, Jobs gained: Workforce transitions in a time of automation. December 2017.

33 L. Gratton, and A. Scott, *The 100-Year Life: living and working in an age of longevity*, London: Bloomsbury, 2016.

34 C. Wu, M. C. Odden, G. G. Fisher, and R. S. Stawski, 'Association of retirement age with mortality: a population based longitudinal study among older adults in the USA', *Journal of Epidemiology and Community Health*, September 2016, 70 (9), 917–23.

35 https://www.manchester.ac.uk/discover/news/unretirement/.

36 It isn't inevitable that higher wages mean more leisure. There is also a substitution effect at work. High wages make leisure expensive and so encourage people to work longer. What happens to leisure depends on the balance of these forces. Over time, to date, it is the income effect (we want more leisure) that has dominated, resulting in declining average hours worked.

37 Huberman and Minns, 'The times they are not changin''.

38 https://www.bbc.co.uk/news/business–48125411.

39 https://www.bls.gov/news.release/conemp.nr0.htm.

40 McKinsey Global Institute, Independent Work: choices, necessity and the gig economy. Manyika, J. Lund, S. Bughin, J. Robinson, K. Mischke, J. and Mahajan, D. October 2016.

41 D. Weil, *'The Fissured Workplace: why work became so bad for so many and what can be done to improve it,* Boston: Harvard University Press, 2019.

42 The philosopher Arthur Schopenhauer put it more colourfully: 'Wealth is like seawater; the more we drink, the thirstier we become.'

43 D. Kahneman, and A. Deaton, 'High income improves evaluation of life but not emotional well-being', *Proceedings of the National Academy of Sciences of the United States of America,* 21 September 2010, Vol. 107 (38), 16489–493.

44 This study inspired Dan Price, CEO of Gravity Payments, to cut his $1million salary to $70,000 and to pay all employees the same amount. We haven't been able to find any press coverage of what this has done to Mr Price's happiness.

CHAPTER FOUR

1 J. J. Arnett, 'Emerging adulthood: a theory of development from the late teens through the twenties', *American Psychologist,* 2000, Vol. 55 (5) 469–80.

2 E. Goffman, *Relations in Public,* London: Allen Lane, 1971.

3 J. Hartshorne, and L. Germine, 'When does cognitive functioning peak? The asynchronous rise and fall of different cognitive abilities across the lifespan', *Psychological Science,* April 2015, 26 (4), 433–43.

4 J. Hartshorne, and L. Germine, 'When does cognitive functioning peak? The asynchronous rise and fall of different cognitive abilities across the lifespan', *Psychological Science,* April 2015, 26 (4), 433–43.

5 Interview with Ignasi Monreal, *FT Weekend,* 3 March 2017.

6 J. Mogensen, 'Cognitive recovery and rehabilitation after brain injury: mechanisms, challenges and support', *Brain Injury: Functional Aspects, Rehabilitation and Prevention,* Croatia: InTech Open Access, 2 March 2012, pp. 121–50, intechopen.com.

7 E. Karle, and C. Pittman, *Rewire Your Anxious Brain: how to use the neuroscience of fear to end anxiety, panic, and worry,* Oakland, CA: New Harbinger Publications, Inc., 2015.

8   S. C. Davies, 'Chief medical officer's summary', in N. Metha, ed., *Annual report of the chief medical officer 2013, public mental health priorities: Investing in the evidence*, [online], London: Department of Health, pp. 11–9; and J. Foster, 'Mental health problems are very common in the workplace – so why don't we talk about it more?,' *Computershare Salary Extras*, 25 November 2015.

9   World Health Organization, *Global burden of mental disorders and the need for a comprehensive, coordinated response from health and social sectors at the country level*, 1 December 2011.

10 E. L. Deci, and R. M. Ryan, 'The "what" and "why" of goal pursuits: human needs and the self-determination of behaviour', *Psychological Inquiry*, 2000, 11: 319–38.

11 Towards Maturity Report, *Preparing for the Future of Learning*. April 2016.

12 G. Petriglieri, S. Ashford, and A. Wrzesniewski, 'Thriving in the Gig Economy', *Harvard Business Review*, March–April 2018.

13 R. Florida, *The Rise of the Creative Class*, New York: Basic Books, 2011.

14 H. Ibarra, *Working Identity: Unconventional Strategies for Reinventing Your Career*, Boston: Harvard Business School Press, 2003.

15 J. E. Marcia, 'Development and validation of ego identity status', *Journal of Personality and Social Psychology*, May 1966, 3 (5), 551–8.

16 E. Wenger, and W. M. Snyder, 'Communities of Practice: the organizational frontier', *Harvard Business Review*, January–February 2000.

17 See, for instance, the summary in Rauch, *The Happiness Curve*.

18 D. Neumark, I. Burn, and P. Button, 'Is it harder for older workers to find jobs? New and improved evidence from a field experiment', NBER Working Paper, 21669, 2016.

19 'How secure is employment at old ages', Urban Institute, December 2018: https://www.urban.org/research/publication/how-secure-employment-older-ages.

20 https://blog.aarp.org/2018/01/05/unemployment-rate-for-those-ages-55-increases-in-december.

21 P. Azowlay, B. Jones, J. Daniel Kim and J. Miranda, 'Age and high-growth entrepreneurship', NBER Working Paper No. 24489, April 2018.

22 M. Nussbaum, and S. Levmore, *Aging Thoughtfully: conversations about retirement, romance, wrinkles and regrets*, Oxford: Oxford University Press, 2017.

23 Nussbaum and Levmore, *Aging Thoughtfully.*

24 D. Kahneman, B. L. Fredrickson, C. A. Schreiber and D. A. Redelmeier, 'When more pain is preferred to less: adding a better end', *Psychological Science*, November 1993, Vol. 4 (6), 401–5.

25 A similar sentiment dominates Atul Gawande's wonderfully humane, *Being Mortal: medicine and what matters in the end*, New York: Picador, Henty Holt and Company, 2017.

26 L. Carstensen, 'Social and emotional patterns in adulthood: support for socioemotional selectivity theory', *Psychology and Aging*, September 1992, Vol. 7 (3), 331–8.

Chapter Five

1 P. Seabright, *The Company of Strangers: a natural history of economic life*, Princeton: Princeton University Press, 2004.

2 https://www.census.gov/data/tables/time-series/demo/families/marital.html.

3 https://www.japantimes.co.jp/news/2017/04/05/national/1-4-japanese-men-still-unmarried-age-50-report/.

4 B. DePaulo, *Singled Out: how singles are stereotyped, stigmatized, and ignored, and still live happily ever after*, New York: St Martin's Griffin, 2006.

5 Lundberg and Pollak, 'The American family and family economics', *Journal of Economic Perspectives*, Vol. 21 (2), 3–26.

6 https://www.nytimes.com/2006/11/02/fashion/02parents.html.

7 https://www.msn.com/en-us/lifestyle/lifestyle-buzz/seven-best-friends-in-china-bought-and-renovated-a-mansion-where-they-intend-to-grow-old-together/ar-AADUaIh?li= BBnb7Kz.

8 Source for Figure 5.1: https://www.brookings.edu/research/lessons-from-the-rise-of-womens-labor-force-participation-in-japan.

9 A. Wolf, *The XX Factor: how working women are creating a new society*, London: Profile Books, 2013.

10 Fifteen per cent of men of working age are not working: 5 per cent are unemployed and 10 per cent are out of the labour force.

11 Quoted in 'Why are so many American men not working?', Alison Burke, https://www.brookings.edu/blog/brookings-now/2017/03/06/why-are-so-many-american-men-not-working/, March 6, 2017

12 K. Gerson, *Hard Choices: how women decide about work, career and motherhood*, California: University of California Press, 1986.

13 A. Giddens, *Modernity and Self-Identity: self and society in the Late Modern Age*, Stanford: Stanford University Press, 1991.

14 J. Stacey, *Brave New Families*, New York: Basic Books, 1990.

15 Stacey, *Brave New Families*.

16 http://www.pewresearch.org/fact-tank/2018/06/13/fathers-day-facts/ft_16-06-14_fathersday_stayathomerising.

17 https://www.oecd.org/dev/development-gender/Unpaid_care_work.pdf.

18 R. Ely, P. Stone, and C. Ammerman, 'Rethink what you "know" about high-achieving women', *Harvard Business Review*, December 2014, 92 (12), 100–09.

19 J. Petriglieri, and O. Obodaru, 'Secure base relationships as drivers of professional identity co-construction in dual career couples', INSEAD Working Paper Series, 2016/04/OBH; and also J. Petriglieri, *Couples that Work: how to thrive in love and work*, Boston: Harvard Business School Press, 2019.

20 M. Strober, *Sharing the Work: what my family and career taught me about breaking through (and holding the door open for others)*, Boston: MIT Press, 2017, p.203

21 N. Ferguson, and E. Freymann, 'The coming generation war', *The Atlantic*, 2019, https://www.theatlantic.com/ideas/archive/2019/05/coming-generation-war/588670.

22 'The French Revolution as it appeared to enthusiasts at its commencement'. William Wordsworth, *The Major Works* (ed) Stephen Gill, Oxford World's Classics, Oxford, July 2008

23 https://www.resolutionfoundation.org/publications/home-affront-housing-across-the-generations.

24 https://www.ft.com/content/b1369286-60f4-11e9-a27a-fdd51850994c.

25 Ipsos Global Trends Survey 2017. https://www.ipsosglobaltrends.com/megatrends-long-term-trends-shaping-the-world-in-2017-and-beyond/

26 https://www.gsb.stanford.edu/faculty-research/publications/beyond-gdp-welfare-across-countries-time.

27 https://voxeu.org/article/how-represent-interests-future-generations-now.

28 N. Howe, and W. Strauss, *Generations*, New York: William Morrow/Quill, 1998.

29 K. Mannheim, 'The problem of generations', *Essays on the Sociology of Knowledge*, London: Routledge and Kegan Paul, 1928/1952, pp. 276–320.

30 D. Costanza, J. Badger, R. Fraser, J. Severt, and P. Gade, 'Generational differences in work-related attitudes: a meta-analysis', *Journal of Business and Psychology*, 2012, Vol. 27, 375–94.

31 L. Gratton, and A. Scott, 'Our assumptions about old and young workers are wrong', *Harvard Business Review*, November 2016: https://hbr.org/2016/11/our-assumptions-about-old-and-young-workers-are-wrong.

32 https://www.pewresearch.org/fact-tank/2018/05/02/millennials-stand-out-for-their-technology-use-but-older-generations-also-embrace-digital-life.

33 R. Luhmann, and L. C. Hawkley, 'Age differences in loneliness from late adolescence to oldest old age', *Developmental Psychology*, 2016, 52 (6), 943–59.

34 Quoted in Brendtro (2006) 'The vision of Urie Bronfenbreenner: Adults who are crazy about kids, Reclaiming Children and Youth: The Journal of Strength-based interventions'.

35 Marc Freedman 'Let's make the most of the intergenerational opportunity', Next Avenue, July 5, 2016, https://www.nextavenue.org/lets-make-intergenerational-opportunity/

36 https://www.marketwatch.com/story/people-spend-more-time-with-facebook-friends-than-with-actual-friends-2016-04-27.

37 https://web.stanford.edu/~mrosenfe/Rosenfeld_et_al_Disintermediating_Friends.pdf.

38 '14th Annual Demographia International Housing Affordability Survey: 2018', http://demographia.com/dhi.pdf.

39 T. Tammaru, M. van Ham, S. Marcinczak, and S. Musterd (eds), '*Socio-Economic Segregation in European Capital Cities*', IZA Discussion Paper 9603, December 2015.

40 See https://www.ageofnoretirement.org/thecommonroom for more details about *The Common Room*.

41 Marc Freedman 'How to Live Forever: The Enduring Power of Connecting the Generations' Public Affairs, November 20, 2018.

42 J. Wilson, 'Volunteering', *Annual Review of Sociology*, Vol. 26, 2000, 215–40.

43 A. Steptoe, A. Shankar, P. Demakakos, and J. Wardle, 'Social isolation, loneliness, and all-cause mortality in older men and women',

Proceedings of the National Academy of Sciences, 2013, 110, 5797–801.

44 P. Boyle, A. Buchman, L. Barnes, and D. Bennett, 'Effect of a purpose in life on risk of incident Alzheimer disease and mild cognitive impairment in community-dwelling older persons', *Archives of General Psychiatry*, 2010, 67, 304–10.

45 P. Boyle, L. Barnes, A. Buchman, D. Bennett, 'Purpose in life is associated with mortality among community-dwelling older persons', *Psychosomatic Medicine*, 2009, 71 (5), 574–9.

46 *A Habit of Service*. 2017 Jubilee Centre for Character and Virtues: University of Birmingham. https://www.jubileecentre. ac.uk/1581/projects/current-projects/a-habit-of-service

47 M. J. Sandel, *What Money Can't Buy, the moral limits of markets*, New York: Farrar, Straus and Giroux, 2012, p. 103.

48 John Rawls, *A Theory of Justice*, Harvard: Harvard University Press, 1971.

49 OECD (2017) 'Preventing Ageing Unequally', OECD Publishing, Paris, 2017.

CHAPTER SIX

1 J. Gotbaum, and B. Wolfe, 2018, 'Help people work longer by phasing retirement', https:www.brookings.edu/opinions/help-people-work-longer-by-phasing-retirement.

2 '18th Annual Transamerica Retirement Survey', https://www. transamericacenter.org/retirement-research/18th-annual-retirement-survey.

3 J. Ameriks, J. Briggs, A. Caplin, M. Lee, M. D. Shapiro, **and** C. Tonetti, 'Older Americans would work longer if jobs were flexible', *American Economic Journal: Macroeconomics*, forthcoming.

4 H. Kleven, C. Landais, J. Posch, A. Steinhauer, and J. Zweimüller, 'Child Penalties Across Countries: Evidence and Explanations', May 2019, AEA Papers and Proceedings, 109, 122–26.

5 C. Goldin, 'A Grand Gender Convergence: its last chapter', *American Economic Review*, 2014, Vol. 104 (4), 1091–119.

6 M. Bertrand, 'The Glass Ceiling', *Economica*, 2018, Vol. 85 (338), 205–31.

7 M. C. Huerta, W. Adema, J. Baxter, H. Wen-Jui, M. Lausten, L. RaeHyuck, and J. Waldfogel, 'Fathers' leave and fathers'

involvement: evidence from four OECD countries', *European Journal of Social Security*, 2014, Vol. 16 (4), 308–46.

8 https://www.personneltoday.com/hr/enhancing-family-friendly-pay-pros-cons.

9 Business in the Community 'Supporting Carers at Work': https://age.bitc.org.uk/sites/default/files/supporting_carers_at_work.pdf.

10 https://www.ft.com/content/6b625a64-9697-11e9-8cfb-30c211dcd229.

11 https://www.oecd.org/dev/development-gender/Unpaid_care_work.pdf.

12 M. Knaus and S. Otterbach, 'Work hour mismatch and job mobility: adjustment channels and resolution rates'. *Economic Inquiry* 57: 227–242.

13 M. Bertrand, 'The Glass Ceiling'.

14 C. Goldin, and L. F. Katz, 'The most egalitarian of professions: pharmacy and the evolution of a family-friendly occupation', *Journal of Labor Economics*, 2016; 34 (3): 705–45.

15 L. Gratton, *The Shift: the future of work is already here*, London: HarperCollins, 2011.

16 McKinsey & Company. 'Coordinating workforce development across stakeholders: An interview with ManpowerGroup CEO Jonas Prising'. Cheng, W.L, Dohrmann, T. and Law, J. October 2018.

17 Bersin by Deloitte: UK learning and development organizations spend less on external training providers, even as budgets rebound. Jan 28th 2016. UK Corporate Learning Factbook 2016: Benchmarks, Trends, and Anaysis of the UK Training Market. Bercon.com

18 https://www.ft.com/content/4fcd2360-8e91-11e8-bb8f-a6a2f7bca546.

19 In conversation with authors.

20 F. Gino, 'The Business Case for Curiosity', *Harvard Business Review*, Sept-Oct, 2018.

21 C. Conley, *Wisdom at Work: the making of a modern elder*, London, Portfolio Penguin, 2018.

22 T. S. Church, D. M. Thomas, C. Tudor-Locke, P. T. Katzmarzyk, C. P. Earnest, R. Q. Rodarte, C. K. Martin, S. N. Blair, and C. Bouchard, 'Trends over 5 decades in US occupation-related physical activities and their associations with obesity', *PlosOne*, 2011, Vol. 6 (5), e196571.

23 A. Borsch-Supan, and M. Weiss, 'Productivity and age: evidence from work teams at the assembly line', *Journal of the Economics of Aging*, 2016, Vol. 7, C, 30–42.

24 A. Duckworth, C. Peterson, M. Matthews, and D. Kelly, 'Grit: perseverance and passion for long-term goals', *Journal of Personality and Social Psychology*, 2007, Vol. 92 (6), 1087–101.

25 https://www.aarp.org/work/job-search/info-2019/mcdonalds-partners-with-aarp.html.

26 J. Birkinshaw, J. Manktelow, V. D'Amato, E. Tosca, and F. Macchi, 'Older and Wise?: how management style varies with age', *MIT Sloan Management Review*, 2019, Vol. 60, 1532–9194.

27 https://www.pwc.com/gx/en/people-organisation/pdf/pwc-preparing-for-tomorrows-workforce-today.pdf.

28 See, as an example, the Bank of America Merrill Lynch report, 'The Silver Dollar – longevity revolution primer': http://www.longfinance.net/programmes/london-accord/la-reports.html?view=report&id=452.

Chapter Seven

1 C. Goldin, and L. Katz, *The Race Between Education and Technology*, Harvard: Harvard University Press, 2010.

2 E. Hoffer, 'Reflections on the Human Condition', Hopewell Publications, 2006.

3 https://www.statista.com/statistics/499431/global-ip-data-traffic-forecast/.

4 'Satya Nadella Talks Microsoft at Middle Age' interview with Dina Bass https://www.bloomberg.com/features/2016-satya-nadella-interview-issue/ August 4, 2016.

5 Angela Ahrendts Quotes. (n.d.). BrainyQuote.com. Retrieved August 13, 2019, from BrainyQuote.com Website: https://www.brainyquote.com/quotes/angela_ahrendts_852654

6 J. Shadbolt, 'Shadbolt Review of Computer Sciences Degree Accreditation and Graduate Employability', https://assets.publishing.service.gov.uk/government/uploads/system/uploads/attachment_data/file/518575/ind-16-5-shadbolt-review-computer-science-graduate-employability.pdf.

7 C. Davidson, *The New Education: how to revolutionize the university to prepare students for a world in flux*, New York: Basic Books, 2017.

8 K. Palmer, and D. Blake, *The Expertise Economy: how the smartest companies use learning to engage, compete and succeed*, Nicholas Brealey Publishing, Boston and London, 2018 p.147.

9 https://pe.gatech.edu/blog/creating-the-next-report.

10 https://dci.stanford.edu

11 P. Beaudry, D. Green, and B. Sand, 'The great reversal in the demand for skill and cognitive tasks', *Journal of Labor Economics*, 2016, Vol. 34 S1(2), S199–247.

12 http://www.cipd.co.uk/publicpolicy/policy-reports/overqualification-skills-mismatch-graduate-labour-market.aspx.

13 Institute for Fiscal Studies, https://www.ifs.org.uk/uploads/publications/bns/BN217.pdf#page=3.

14 A. Scott, 'Education, Age and the Machine', in C. Dede, and J. Richards (eds), *The 60 Year Curriculum: new models for lifelong learning in the digital economy*, forthcoming Routledge, 2020.

15 K. Palmer and D. Blake, *The Expertise Economy: How the smartest companies use learning to engage, compete and succeed*, Nicholas Brealey Publishing, Boston and London, 2018 p.147.

16 D. Deming, 'The growing importance of social skills in the labour market', *Quarterly Journal of Economics* 2017, Vol. 132, 4, 1593–640.

17 L. Gratton, 'The challenges of scaling soft skills', *MIT Sloan Management Review*, 6 August 2018.

18 L. Gratton, 'New frontiers in re-skilling and up-skilling', *MIT Sloan Management Review*, 8 July 2019.

19 https://www.gov.uk/government/publications/adult-participation-in-learning-survey-2017.

20 Named after Google's chief economist Hal Varian https://en.wikipedia.org/wiki/Varian_Rule.

21 In the UK, an MOT (originally Ministry of Transport) test is the annual inspection of cars over three years old that takes an audit of their condition and whether they are roadworthy and requiring remedial action in the case of failures. Without an MOT the car cannot be legally driven on the roads.

22 McKinsey Global Institute Report, 2017, 'Jobs lost, jobs gained', https://www.mckinsey.com/featured-insights/future-of-work/jobs-lost-jobs-gained-what-the-future-of-work-will-mean-for-jobs-skills-and-wages.

23 Quoted in C. Davidson, *The New Education: how to revolutionize the university to prepare students for a world in flux*, New York: Basic Books, 2017, p. 127.

24 'Harvard's dean of continuing education pushes educational frontier', Nancy Duvergne Smith, MIT Technology Review, 21 October, 2014, https://www.technologyreview.com/s/531381/huntington-lambert-sm-85/

CHAPTER EIGHT

1 L. Nedelkoska and G. Quintini (2018), 'Automation, skills use and training', OECD Social, Employment and Migration Working Papers No. 202, OECD Publishing, Paris.

2 OECD, 'Basic Income as a Policy Option', May 2017, OECD Social, Employment and Migration Working Papers No. 202, OECD Publishing, Paris.

3 OECD, 'Basic Income as a Policy Option'.

4 https://www.weforum.org/agenda/2019/04/where-do-good-jobs-come-from/.

5 O. Mitchell, J. Poterba, M. Warshawsky, and J. Brown, 'New Evidence on the Money's Worth of Individual', *Annuities American Economic Review*, 1999, 89(5), 1299–318.

6 N. Kassebaum, et al, 'Global, regional and national disability adjusted life years for 315 diseases and injuries and healthy life expectancy, 1990–2015: a systematic analysis for the Global Burden of Disease Study', 2015, *The Lancet*, 2016; 388, 10053, P1603–658.

7 James Fries of Stanford University, http://aramis.stanford.edu/downloads/1980FriesNEJM130.pdf.

8 S. Jay Olshansky, 'From lifespan to healthspan', *Journal of American Medical Association*, October 2018, 320(13): 1323–1324.

9 https://voxeu.org/article/does-aging-really-affect-health-expenditures-if-so-why.

10 https://www.kvpr.org/post/delaying-aging-may-have-bigger-payoff-fighting-disease.

11 Speaking at The Longevity Forum, November 2018, London.

12 'Towards more physical activity: transforming public spaces to promote physical activity – a key contributor to achieving the Sustainable Development Goals in Europe', World Health Organisation, 2017.

13 J. Beard, and D. Bloom, 'Towards a comprehensive public health response to population aging', *The Lancet*, 2015, Vol. 385 (9968), 658–61.

14 R. Barrell, S. Kirby, and A. Orazgani, 'The macroeconomic impact from extending working lives', Department for Work and Pensions Working Paper, 95, 2011.

15 See D. Coyle, *GDP: a brief but affectionate history*, Princeton: Princeton University Press, 2014, for a highly readable history and evaluation.

16 https://www.nzherald.co.nz/business/news/article.cfm?c_id=3&objectid=11993716.

IMAGE CREDITS

INDEX

Page numbers in **bold** refer to figures.

233

A NOTE ON THE AUTHORS

Andrew J. Scott is Professor of Economics at the London Business School and consulting scholar at Stanford University's Center on Longevity, having previously held positions at Harvard and Oxford. Through his multi-award-winning research, writing and teaching, his ideas inform a global understanding of the profound shifts reshaping our world and the actions needed for us to flourish individually and as a society. Board member and advisor to a range of corporates and governments, he is co-founder of the Longevity Forum and a member of the advisory board of the Office for Budget Responsibility and the UK Cabinet Office Honours Committee.

Lynda Gratton is Professor of Management Practice at the London Business School, where she received the Excellence in Teaching Award in 2015 and directs the highly acclaimed course on the Future of Work. Lynda sits as a steward on the World Economic Forum's Council on the New Education and Work Agenda and has attended Davos since 2013. She is ranked by Thinkers50 as one of the top fifteen business thinkers in the world, and in 2018 was appointed by Prime Minister Shinzo Abe to be a member of his Council for Designing the 100-Year Life Society.

A NOTE ON THE TYPE

The text of this book is set in Linotype Sabon, a typeface named after the type founder, Jacques Sabon. It was designed by Jan Tschichold and jointly developed by Linotype, Monotype and Stempel in response to a need for a typeface to be available in identical form for mechanical hot metal composition and hand composition using foundry type.

Tschichold based his design for Sabon roman on a font engraved by Garamond, and Sabon italic on a font by Granjon. It was first used in 1966 and has proved an enduring modern classic.

A practical guide to how we can flourish as longevity and technology change our world, from the internationally bestselling authors of *The 100-Year Life*.

Smart new technologies. Longer, healthier lives. Human progress has risen to great heights, but at the same time it has prompted anxiety about where we're heading. Are our jobs under threat? If we live to 100, will we ever really stop working? And how will this change the way we love, manage and learn from others?

One thing is clear: advances in technology have not been matched by the necessary innovation to our social structures. In our era of unprecedented change, we haven't yet discovered new ways of living.

Drawing from the fields of economics and psychology, Andrew J. Scott and Lynda Gratton offer a simple framework based on three fundamental principles (Narrate, Explore and Relate) to give you the tools to navigate the challenges ahead. *The New Long Life* is the essential guide to a longer, smarter, happier life.